Shire County G

NOTTINGHAMSHIRE

Jeff and Margaret Hopewell

Shire Publications Ltd

Printed in Great Britain by CIT Printing Services, Press Buildings, Merlins Bridge, Haverfordwest, Dyfed SA61 1XF.

British Library Cataloguing in Publication Data:
Hopewell, Jeffery
    Nottinghamshire. - (Shire County Guides; No. 35)
    I. Title II. Hopewell, Margaret
    III. Series
    914. 25204
    ISBN   0-7478-0194-0

Cover: Newark Castle and the river Trent.

Acknowledgements

Photographs are acknowledged as follows: Jeff Hopewell, pages 9, 11, 13, 16, 17, 42, 53, 57 (upper), 59, 61, 67, 83, 94, 96, 97, 99, 100 (left), 103 and 109 (left); Cadbury Lamb, pages 14, 19, 22, 26, 28, 29, 32, 34, 35, 43, 46, 50, 51, 55, 57 (lower), 62, 71, 74, 79, 82, 88, 89, 91, 93 (upper), 100 (right), 102, 104, 109 (right) and 112; Newark Museum, pages 10, 20, 25 and 87; Nottinghamshire County Council Leisure Services, cover picture and pages 33, 36, 37, 40, 41, 45, 48, 65, 69, 73, 76 and 80; Nottingham Evening Post, pages 93 (lower) and 116; The Story of Nottingham Lace, page 77 (upper); The Tales of Robin Hood, page 77 (lower). The maps were produced by Robert Dizon.

Ordnance Survey grid references

Although information on how to reach most of the places described in this book by car is given in the text, National Grid References are also included in many instances, particularly for the harder-to-find places in chapters 3, 4 and 8. For the benefit of those readers who have the Ordnance Survey 1:50,000 Landranger maps of the area the references are stated as a Landranger sheet number followed by the 100 km National Grid square and the six-figure reference.

To locate a site by means of the grid references, proceed as in the following example: Bestwood Country Park (OS   129: SK 572463). Take the OS Landranger map sheet 129 ('Nottingham, Loughborough and surrounding area'). The grid numbers are printed in blue around the edges of the map. (In more recently produced maps these numbers are repeated at 10 km intervals throughout the map, so that it is not necessary to open it out completely.) Read off these numbers from the left along the top edge of the map until you come to 57, denoting a vertical grid line, then estimate two-tenths of the distance to vertical line 58 and envisage an imaginary vertical grid line 57.2 at this point. Next look at the grid numbers at one side of the map (either side will do) and read *upwards* until you find the horizontal grid line 46. Estimate three-tenths of the distance to the next horizontal line above (i.e. 47), and so envisage an imaginary horizontal line across the map at 46.3. Follow this imaginary line across the map until it crosses the imaginary vertical line 57.2. At the intersection of these two lines you will find Bestwood Country Park.

The Ordnance Survey Landranger maps which cover Nottinghamshire are sheets 111, 120, 121 and 129, with very small areas on 112 and 130.

Contents

PLACES TO VISIT IN NOTTINGHAMSHIRE

- ■ Towns and villages (chapter 2)
- 🇮 Towns and villages with information centre (chapters 2 and 13)
- 🏃 Countryside (chapter 3)
- ⊓ Ancient monuments (chapter 4)
- † Churches (chapter 5)
- 🏛 Historic buildings and gardens (chapter 6)
- 🏛 Museums (chapter 7)
- ⚒ Industrial archaeology (chapter 8)
- ○ Other places to visit (chapter 9)
- ● Other places
- 🇮 Tourist information centre (chapter 13)
- === Principal road

0   5   15 kilometres
0   10 miles

DONCASTER
HUMBERSIDE
SOUTH YORKSHIRE
Bawtry
West Stockwith
Gringley on the Hill
GAINSBOROUGH
Langold Country Park & Dyscarr Wood
Mattersey Priory
Blyth
Daneshill Lakes
Littleborough toll cottage
Hodsock Priory Gardens
Wetlands Waterfowl Reserve
Littleborough
North Leverton windmill
Carlton in Lindrick
Clarborough Tunnel
RETFORD
WORKSOP
Hannah Park Wood
Eaton Wood
Sundown Kiddies Adventureland
Clumber Park
Bothamsall Castle
East Markham
Kingshaugh
Fledborough
Dukeries Adv. Pk
Creswell Crags
Cuckney Castle
World of Robin Hood
Longbottoms Mill
Tuxford
Pureland Japanese Garden
LINCOLN
CHESTERFIELD
DERBYSHIRE
BOLSOVER
Sherwood Forest Country Park
Kirton Wood
Egmanton
Spalford Warren
Warsop
Ollerton
Ollerton watermill
Laxton
Sutton on Trent
Edwinstowe
Wellow
Carlton-on-Trent
South Scarle
Meden Trail
King John's Palace
Ossington
Collingham
Spa Ponds
Clipstone Forest
Rufford Country Park & Abbey
Norwell
Vina Cooke Museum of Dolls
MANSFIELD
Winkburn
Holme by Newark
SUTTON IN ASHFIELD
British Horological Institute
Newark Air Museum
KIRKBY IN ASHFIELD
ALFRETON
Blidworth
Reg Taylor's Swan Sanctuary
Kelham
Coddington
Halam
Averham
NEWARK
RIPLEY
SOUTHWELL
Fiskerton Mill
Queen's Sconce
Barnby in the Willows dovecote
HUCKNALL
Oxton
Hawton
EASTWOOD
Epperstone
Bleasby dovecote
Gonalston
Thurgarton
Sibthorpe dovecote
Hawksworth
Staunton in the Vale
ILKESTON
Car Colston
Thoroton dovecote
Scarrington
NOTTINGHAM
Cranmer's Mound
LINCOLNSHIRE
Bingham
Whatton
DERBY
BEESTON
Wild Flower Farm
GRANTHAM
Attenborough
Clifton
Langar
LONG EATON
Bunny
Kingston on Soar
East Leake
Sutton Bonington
See page 5 for enlargement of this area
LEICESTERSHIRE
LOUGHBOROUGH
MELTON MOWBRAY

N

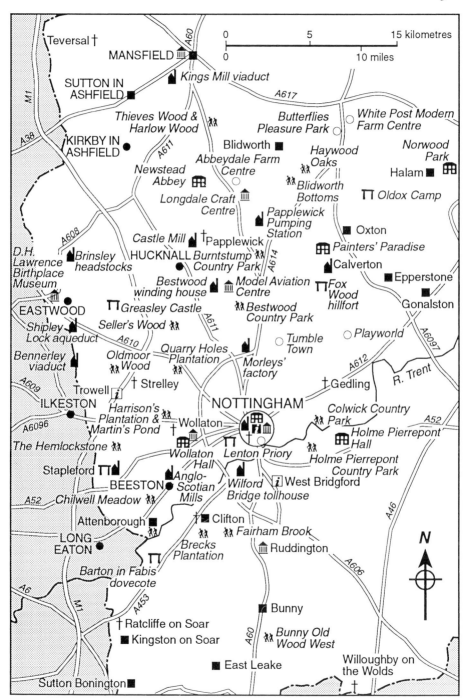

Teversal †

MANSFIELD

Kings Mill viaduct

SUTTON IN
ASHFIELD

A617

*Thieves Wood &
Harlow Wood*

*Butterflies
Pleasure Park*

*White Post Modern
Farm Centre*

KIRKBY IN
ASHFIELD

A611

Blidworth

*Haywood
Oaks*

*Norwood
Park*

Halam

*Abbeydale Farm
Centre*

*Newstead
Abbey*

*Blidworth
Bottoms*

Π *Oldox Camp*

*Longdale Craft
Centre*

*Papplewick
Pumping
Station*

Castle Mill † *Papplewick*

Oxton

D.H.
Lawrence
Birthplace
Museum

*Brinsley
headstocks*

HUCKNALL

*Burntstump
Country Park*

A614

Painters' Paradise

Calverton

Epperstone

*Bestwood
winding house*

*Model Aviation
Centre*

Π*Fox
Wood
hillfort*

Gonalston

EASTWOOD

Π *Greasley Castle*

*Bestwood
Country Park*

A6097

*Shipley
Lock aqueduct*

Seller's Wood

A611

*Tumble
Town*

Playworld

*Bennerley
viaduct*

*Oldmoor
Wood*

*Quarry Holes
Plantation*

*Morleys'
factory*

A612

R. Trent

A609

Trowell

† *Strelley*

† Gedling

ILKESTON

*Harrison's
Plantation &
Martin's Pond*

Wollaton

NOTTINGHAM

*Colwick Country
Park*

A52

A6096

A610

The Hemlockstone

*Wollaton
Hall*

Lenton Priory

*Holme Pierrepont
Hall*

*Holme Pierrepont
Country Park*

Stapleford

Π

*Anglo-
Scotian
Mills*

*Wilford
Bridge tollhouse*

West Bridgford

A46

A52

BEESTON

Chilwell Meadow

Attenborough

† ■ *Clifton*

Fairham Brook

LONG
EATON

*Brecks
Plantation*

Ruddington

A606

*Barton in Fabis
dovecote*

A6

M1

A453

Bunny

A60

*Bunny Old
Wood West*

N

† *Ratcliffe on Soar*

Kingston on Soar

*Willoughby on
the Wolds*

East Leake

Sutton Bonington

†

0   5   15 kilometres
0   10 miles

Preface

Welcome to the Shire County Guide to Nottinghamshire, one of over thirty such books, written and designed to enable you to organise your time in each county well.

The Shire County Guides fill the need for a compact, accurate and thorough guide to each county so that visitors can plan a half-day excursion or a whole week's stay to best advantage. Residents, too, will find the guides a handy and reliable reference to the places of interest in their area.

Travelling British roads can be time consuming, and Shire County Guides will ensure that you need not inadvertently miss any interesting feature in a locality, that you do not accidentally bypass a new museum or an outstanding church, that you can find an attractive place to picnic, and that you will appreciate the history and the buildings of the towns or villages in which you stop.

This book has been arranged in special interest chapters, such as the countryside, historic buildings or ancient monuments, and all these places of interest are located on the map on pages 4-5. Use the map either for an overview to decide which area has most to interest you, or to help you enjoy your immediate neighbourhood. Then refer to the nearest town or village in chapter 2 'Nottinghamshire towns and villages' to see, at a glance, what special features or attractions each community contains or is near. The subsequent chapters enable readers with a particular interest to find immediately those places of importance to them, while the cross-referencing under 'Nottingham-shire towns and villages' assists readers with wider tastes to select how best to spend their time.

1
Nottinghamshire: the romance and the reality

The chances are that the first things that spring to mind about Nottinghamshire are Robin Hood and Sherwood Forest, and D. H. Lawrence and coal mining. The former speak of legends and films, and the latter of hard labour and grime, summing up between them the contrasts of the county — the romance and the reality. The other famous product of Nottingham, its lace, encapsulates both, with the delicate fabric being made in former times in intolerable working conditions. With the city and industrialised towns on the one hand and ancient market towns and remote rural villages on the other, Nottinghamshire can cater for most people's interests.

The county divides up geologically into three broad north-south strips: Permian rocks to the west, Bunter sandstone in the centre and Keuper sandstone and marl to the east with the river Trent flowing along it. Just west of Nottingham are the coal measures and to the south-east are Lias stone and clays. There is good building stone in the county: Mansfield sandstone and Magnesian limestone, and to a lesser extent Blue Lias and skerry. Although there were plenty of oaks in Sherwood, these belonged to the King, so timber-framed buildings are comparatively rare; the best examples are at Newark and Southwell. Brick is the most common building material, found as early as 1500 at Holme Pierrepont but not widely used until the mid seventeenth century. The Victorians preferred slates for roofing, but before that pantiles were the norm.

Creswell Crags is the best-known prehistoric site in the county; otherwise most early evidence of human occupation comes from finds of flint tools along the Trent valley. Similarly most bronze age weapons have been found within a few miles of the river, for example at Attenborough, Gotham, Clifton, Nottingham, Holme Pierrepont, Fiskerton and

Newark, though an early bronze age flat axe was discovered at Mansfield Woodhouse. Iron age settlements or hillforts are mainly in a group north of Nottingham: Lodge Farm (Burton Joyce), Fox Wood (Woodborough), Oldox (Oxton) and Combs Farm (Farnsfield). Leeming Lane, from Mansfield to Warsop, is an ancient trackway of the same period and Stone Street, running from Nottingham to Blyth, may be just as early. Sewstern Lane, starting at Stamford (Lincolnshire), does not touch the county until almost at its destination, Newark, but there are two branches — one that crosses the boundary between Harby (Leicestershire) and Colston Bassett on its way to Nottingham, and another known as Long Hedge Lane, which enters the county between Bottesford (Leicestershire) and Alverton, arriving at Hazelford Ferry on the Trent.

The most famous Roman road is the Fosse Way, the modern A46. It ran from Exeter to Lincoln, entering Nottinghamshire in the south and leaving north-east of Newark. There were at least four forts along the road: Vernemetum (Willoughby on the Wolds), Margidunum (East Bridgford), Ad Pontem (East Stoke) and Crocolana (Brough). From Ad Pontem a minor road led north-east. Its course can quite easily be traced, particularly through Southwell, as far as the Edingley-Kirklington road, where it disappears. The other major road was the Till Bridge Lane, from Lincoln to Doncaster, which crossed the Trent, possibly by a pontoon bridge, at Segelocum (Littleborough) and went west to what is now Bawtry. Some fifteen Roman villas have been discovered, notably at Mansfield Woodhouse, first excavated in 1786, and at Southwell, now under the Minster, though some of its mosaic and wall plaster can be seen. A Romano-Celtic temple has been found at Red Hill, Ratcliffe on Soar.

In Anglo-Saxon times the county seems to have been claimed by the kings of both Mercia and Northumbria. Edwin, the Christian king of Northumbria, defeated his predecessor, Aethelfrith, in 617 near the river Idle in the north of Nottinghamshire. Bede records the baptism of many of Edwin's followers in the Trent near Tiovulfingacestir, identified variously as Littleborough, Southwell or Treswell. Edwin himself was canonised as a martyr when he died fighting against Penda, king of Mercia, in 633 at the battle of Heathfield, near Cuckney. Anglo-Saxon place-names are found throughout the county. Those ending in -ing, -ingham and -ington are probably the earliest, for example Gedling, Nottingham and Kirklington. Later endings are -ton and -worth, for example Carlton (the farm of the peasants) and Awsworth. More tangible evidence comes from burial sites, either of funerary urns as at Newark, Kingston on Soar and Sutton Bonington, or of corpses as at Aslockton, Bingham and Cotgrave.

The Danes arrived at Nottingham in 867 and at the Treaty of Wedmore, signed in 878, the county became part of the Danelaw, changing hands several times until the Danes were finally defeated in 942. They too left their mark in place-names, especially those ending in -by and -thorpe, such as Skegby and Caythorpe. When the Anglo-Saxons re-asserted themselves and times were a little more peaceful they were able to build, or rebuild, their churches. The tower of Carlton in Lindrick church is the best example of the period, along with the fine cross at Stapleford.

With the Norman conquest in 1066 both Saxon and Danish landowners were displaced or perhaps became tenants on the land that had once belonged to them. The King himself was a substantial landowner; the other major figure was Roger de Busli, who owned 107 manors. William Peverel held 49 manors and was given the Honour of Nottingham, a feudal privilege, under which he built the castle. The Archbishop of York owned much land, especially around Southwell, and the Bishop of Lincoln was lord of the manor of Newark. Sherwood Forest accounted for about 20 per cent of the county, some 160 square miles (414 sq km), and was governed by forest laws upheld by the verderers at courts held every six weeks at Linby, and similarly at Calverton, Mansfield and Edwinstowe. Until the system declined in the fourteenth century they dealt with cases of poaching and felling trees or grazing cattle without authorisation. Imprisonment and fines were the usual penalties though in early Norman times blinding and mutilation were not uncommon sentences. Outlaws, such as Robin Hood, lived dangerously!

Nottingham and its castle were captured and recaptured several times between 1140 and 1153 in the civil war between Stephen and Matilda. In a rebellion against Henry II in 1174 the town was plundered by William de Ferrers, Earl of Derby, and in 1194 the castle was held by John's supporters against Richard I, though they surrendered after a siege of only three days. John, as king, frequently came to Nottingham and died of dysentery at Newark. In the Barons' War, when Simon de Montfort, Earl of Leicester, rose against Henry III, Nottingham Castle changed hands more than once. The town's walls were not built until about 1267. They ran north-west from the castle, curving right along what is now Park Row and continuing along Upper and Lower Parliament Streets almost as far as Southwell Road. On the southern side the town seems to have relied on natural defences. The main industries of the town in the middle ages were pottery, bellfounding and alabaster carving. Statues of saints and panels of religious scenes were sold throughout England and exported as far as Iceland and Spain. The Castle Museum has a fine collection — apparently images of John the Baptist's head on a charger were a particular speciality.

Most religious houses in the county were founded in the twelfth century and at the time of the Dissolution there were sixteen. In addition to those mentioned elsewhere in the text — Lenton, Newstead, Rufford, Thurgarton, Worksop, Blyth and Mattersey — there were nine more: Beauvale and Felley Priories (both west of Hucknall), Welbeck Abbey, Shelford Priory, nunneries at Wallingwells (near Carlton in Lindrick) and Broadholme, two friaries at Nottingham for the Franciscans and Carmelites and one at Newark for the Observant Friars, which was founded as late as 1507 by Henry VII. Most were supported by the revenues of land given to them by benefactors or by clearing and farming land themselves, though Beauvale gained additional income by granting leases for mining coal on its property. At the Dissolution all passed into the hands of secular landowners.

Other than the death of Queen Eleanor at Harby in 1290 and the capture of Mortimer, Queen Isabella's lover, by Edward III at Nottingham Castle in 1327, little of national importance happened in the county until the Wars of the Roses. It was on 11th August 1485, whilst at his hunting lodge at Bestwood, that Richard III heard of Henry Tudor's landing at Milford Haven, and it was from Nottingham that he marched to his death at Bosworth eleven days later. In 1487 Henry was himself threatened by the pretender Lambert Simnel. Their armies met at East Stoke on 16th June and between six and seven thousand soldiers died that day before Henry was victorious. Many of the rebels were killed as they fled to cross the Trent and a nearby ditch is called Red Gutter, supposedly from the blood that flowed in it.

Church affairs came into prominence in the sixteenth century throughout England as well as in Nottinghamshire. It was only in his disgrace in 1530 that Cardinal Wolsey, Archbishop of York, ever set foot in his diocese, spending four months at Southwell and another month at Scrooby, not long before his death at Leicester Abbey. Thomas Cranmer, another major figure in the Tudor church, was born at Aslockton and is now remembered as one of the outstanding Archbishops of Canterbury, who shaped the Book of Common Prayer and died at the stake. The Reformation did not go far enough for some and Scrooby figures again in history as the meeting place of the leaders of the Pilgrim Fathers.

Religious differences were a contributory factor in the Civil War. It was at Nottingham that Charles I raised his standard on 22nd August 1642, but the town's loyalty was not strong and Newark became the main Royalist stronghold in the county. The nobility mostly supported the King whilst the local gentry were generally on the side of Parliament. Families were divided on the issue. Robert Pierrepont, first Earl of Kingston upon Hull, tried unsuccessfully to remain neutral, but his eldest son fought for the Cavaliers whereas his two younger sons were with the opposition. No major battles were fought in the county but there were a number of skirmishes and Nottingham and Newark were frequently besieged. Several country houses were captured or recaptured during the war — Welbeck, Newstead, Staunton, Wiverton, Thurgarton, Norwell and Shelford, which was destroyed as a result. The war ended with the surrender of Charles I at Southwell on 5th May 1646.

Under Charles II the nobility were back in the ascendant, and the northern part of Sherwood Forest gradually became swallowed up into the estates of several dukes, hence the nickname of the 'Dukeries'. Three were descended from Bess of Hardwick: the Dukes of Kingston, who held Thoresby; the Dukes

West Burton power station seen from the ruined church at South Wheatley.

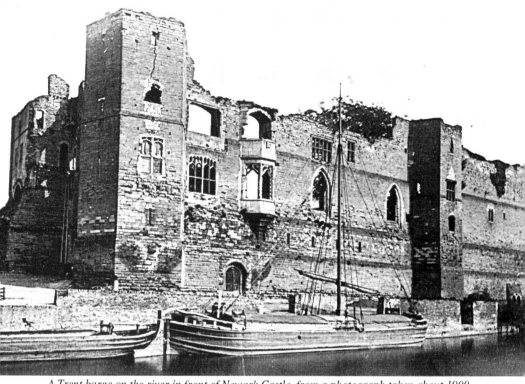

A Trent barge on the river in front of Newark Castle, from a photograph taken about 1900.

of Newcastle, owners of Clumber and Welbeck; and the Dukes of Norfolk, of Worksop Manor. Rufford is usually considered part of the Dukeries although it was owned by a nobleman of lesser rank than a duke, the Marquess of Halifax.

It was in the later seventeenth century that framework knitting became a major industry, especially around Nottingham itself, where the medieval pottery trade still continued, along with glass-blowing. As time went on these last two declined whereas hosiery manufacture went from strength to strength, to be joined later by the city's most famous product, lace. Celia Fiennes noted the local manufacture of brick in her travels in 1697. Most of the bricks used to build Nottingham were made nearby, and even St Pancras station in London was made of Mapperley brick. The county is well known for its coalfields. The first documentary record is of mining at Cossall in 1282, though it is known that the Romans used coal over a thousand years earlier. This would have been open-cast or shallow mining for it was not until 1859 that

the first deep pit was sunk at Shireoaks.

The Trent was from earliest times used for transporting merchandise to and fro, but trade was much increased with improvements at Newark in 1773 and along the whole length of the river in the county 21 years later. In 1777 the Chesterfield Canal was opened, joining the Trent at West Stockwith. The Erewash Canal opened in 1779, benefiting the coal industry, and its competitor, the Nottingham Canal, came into use in 1796. A year later, in the last outbreak of 'canal fever', the Nottingham to Grantham canal was finished.

It was not long before 'railway mania' became the rage. The first steam train ran from Derby to Nottingham in 1839 at a top speed of 40 mph (64 km/h) on the Midland Counties Railway line. Thereafter new companies were formed and lines opened at a rapid pace. The county was soon criss-crossed by railways and served by around 140 stations. Nottingham's Midland Station survives but the equally impressive Victoria Station, built in 1898-1900 for the Great Central Railway, has gone. 1300 houses were demolished to provide a suitable site but it was pulled down in its turn some seventy years later and replaced by a shopping precinct. 'Railway mania' has given way to 'motorway madness', though the M1 is the sole motorway in the county and only 12 miles (19 km) of that lie within the boundary.

Nottingham became a city in 1897 and with its traditional industries in decline in the twentieth century it is as well that others sprang up to take their place. Some of them became household names. John Player set up in business as an agent for manure and seeds, selling tobacco as a sideline. He quickly saw potential in ready-rolled cigarettes, bought a local tobacco factory in 1877 and was so successful that he opened his Castle Factory in 1884. As part of Imperial Tobacco, the firm employed as many as 7500 people by the mid 1930s. Jesse Boot was a local lad, who in 1863 left school to work in his mother's herbalist shop; by a policy of buying in bulk to be able to sell at a discount, he built up a chain of shops and started manufacturing on a large scale. He was a great benefactor to the city, as well as providing employment. In 1868 Thomas Humber set up as a bicycle manufacturer in Nottingham, moving to Beeston with a workforce of eighty in 1880. Eighteen years later the firm employed 1800 people. It had branched out into motorcycles and by 1903 motorcars as well, but the whole operation was moved to Coventry in 1908. It was, however, Raleigh that became the foremost name in cycling. In 1886 Woodhead, Angois and Ellis had formed a partnership producing three cycles a week in a workshop near Raleigh Street, Nottingham. The next year

Frank Bowden was sent home from Hong Kong by his doctors, who were expecting him to die. Instead he took up cycling and was so enthusiastic that a year later he traced the makers of his tricycle and bought them out. By 1896 he had built up the largest cycle factory in the world at Lenton.

Two industries are relative newcomers. The power stations along the Trent valley have sprung up only since 1945 and can be seen from many miles away. Less obvious, and on a much smaller scale, is the Nottinghamshire oilfield. The first successful drilling was at Eakring in 1939 and during the Second World War the supply of oil from these wells was particularly valuable. The only sign above ground of their existence is a nodding-donkey pump.

Other household names are in the realm of sport. Nottinghamshire County Cricket Club was founded at Trent Bridge in 1841 and still plays on the same ground. Both Notts County and Nottingham Forest football clubs, founded in 1862 and 1865 respectively, used the cricket ground in the nineteenth century until they got their own grounds. Curiously Notts County has its ground in the city and Nottingham Forest in the county.

With racecourses at Southwell and Nottingham, the Trent for anglers, Holme Pierrepont for water sports and plenty of country parks and trails there is no shortage of leisure facilities. Tourism is on the increase and with the Center Parcs complex in Sherwood Forest, more people are spending holidays in the county. Both locals and those from further afield will find much to enjoy in Nottinghamshire.

An early Humber trademark on the company's former factory in Beeston.

2
Nottinghamshire towns and villages

Arnold

Burntstump Country Park, page 47; Tumble Town, page 106.

Aslockton

Cranmer's Mound, page 56.

Attenborough

The former gravel pits of Attenborough have become a nature reserve, but in the past they not only were a source of materials and employment but also yielded archaeological finds going back to Roman times and even earlier. The church, dedicated to St Mary Magdalen, dates from the Norman period, as indicated by a blocked door on the north side and twelfth-century coffin slabs in the south porch with its equally ancient door. The nave is thirteenth-century, though the capitals of the pillars, with their curious heads, were recarved in the following century, possibly at the same time as the aisles were widened and the tower built. The steeple was added in the fifteenth century, as was the clerestory, to increase the height of the nave and admit more light. There are some interesting fittings: a plain thirteenth-century font, two fourteenth-century bench ends, some secular Jacobean woodwork in the choirstalls and a Jacobean communion table. The royal arms of George IV are hung here as well as two hatchments, one of which displays the arms of Admiral Sir John Borlase Warren, of Stapleford, who was a Member of Parliament for Nottingham from 1796 to 1806, defeated the French fleet in 1798 and was later ambassador to Russia. Several pubs in the county are named after him. Just west of the church is Ireton House, birthplace of Henry Ireton (page 114).

Attenborough Gravel Pits, page 50.
In the locality: Chilwell Meadow, page 51;

Anglo-Scotian Mills, page 96.

Averham

In Nottinghamshire the letter V in place-names tends to be dropped in pronunciation, so Averham becomes 'Airam'. Although overshadowed by Staythorpe power station, it is a pleasant village, especially as one walks towards the church and rectory by the river Trent. The church, St Michael, was built in the twelfth century and characteristic herringbone masonry may be seen in the tower, nave and chancel. Three hundred years later the chancel was extended, new windows were made and the tower was given buttresses and a further storey with battlements, pinnacles and gargoyles. Sir Thomas Sutton had the south porch built early in the sixteenth century, and his arms and initials were carved on it. There are monuments to earlier Suttons in the church, but that to Sir William Sutton (died 1611) and his wife outshines the rest, with its fine alabaster effigies and colourful heraldry. Opposite is the wall monument to his son Robert, created first Lord Lexington by Charles I in recognition of his fund-raising activities for the Royalist cause. His manor house was destroyed by the Parliamentarians, though the moated site can be seen on the right-hand side of the lane leading to the church. He lived until 1668, long enough to see the Restoration, but Kelham became the family home (page 21). The family retained local connections, however, and his son built Averham Park House as a hunting lodge.

A later Sutton, Charles, was rector of Averham for 51 years, dying in 1785, when he was followed by his son, Charles Manners Sutton, who also became Archbishop of Canterbury, but held the living for only 43 years. The two hatchments are to his successor, the Reverend Robert Chaplin (died 1837), and his wife, who was a Sutton. Another of the family, Canon F. H. Sutton, of Brant Broughton, Lincolnshire, put together the windows of ancient glass. A later rector, Joseph Walker, was here for 51 years until his death in 1907, when he was succeeded by his son, Cyril Walker, who built the Robin Hood Theatre in the grounds of the early Victorian rectory. Sir Donald Wolfit (1902-68), born at nearby Balderton, made his acting debut here, and the theatre is still used regularly.

In Pinfold Lane is a small brick building with a stable door. It might be mistaken for a privy but the chimney at the back indicates that it was the parish oven.

In the locality: British Horological Institute, page 95.

Awsworth
Bennerley viaduct, page 96.

Barnby in the Willows
Barnby in the Willows dovecote, page 56.

Barton in Fabis
Barton in Fabis dovecote, page 56.

Beeston
Anglo-Scotian Mills, page 96.
In the locality: Attenborough Gravel Pits, page 50; Chilwell Meadow, page 51; The Hemlockstone, page 52; Stapleford church cross, page 62; Stapleford framework knitters' cottages, page 102.

Bestwood
Bestwood Country Park, page 47; Model Aviation Centre, page 85; Bestwood winding house, page 97.

Bingham
Early closing, Wednesday; market day, Thursday.
After a period of decline in the nineteenth century, Bingham is once again a thriving market town, gradually creeping nearer Nottingham from its medieval site east of the church. Apart from the brick Manor House of about 1700, most of the buildings in the Market Place are Victorian, as is the Butter Cross, which was erected to the memory of John Hassall, Lord Chesterfield's agent. The church, All Saints, does not adjoin the Market Place but lies further east. The lower stage of the tower dates from the thirteenth century, with the upper stage finished by about 1300. The broach spire with lucarnes was added in the following century. At the corners of the tower are two pinnacles and two statues of bishops. The pillars in the nave are early fourteenth-century and have interesting capitals carved with leaves, animals and a variety of ugly heads. Most of the glass and fittings are nineteenth- or early twentieth-century, but the font is Norman. A former rector of Bingham, George Abbot, became Archbishop of Canterbury, but his only memorable achievement whilst in office was in 1621 when he aimed his crossbow at a deer but killed a gamekeeper instead.

In the locality: Cranmer's Mound, page 56; Thoroton dovecote, page 62; churches at Langar, page 66 and Whatton, page 74; Wild Flower Farm Visitors Centre, page 106.

Averham: the village oven.

Blyth: the former rectory and church.

Bleasby

Bleasby dovecote, page 56.

Blidworth

What was once a small forest village changed dramatically with the opening of the colliery in 1925 and may change again following its closure in 1988. The old village is on a hill, south-west of the pit. Some of the cottages are older than the church, which, with the exception of the much restored fifteenth-century tower, was built in a classical style in 1739. It has the unusual dedication of St Mary of the Purification, hence its unique annual Rocking Ceremony. On the Sunday nearest 2nd February, the Feast of the Presentation of Christ in the Temple, the boy born closest to Christmas Day the previous year is put into the eighteenth-century cradle and rocked gently in it, whilst appropriate prayers are said. There are several unusual features in the church. The early nineteenth-century pulpit came from Southwell Minster, as did the Jacobean panelling in the chancel. A psalm board, precursor of the hymn board, displays on the reverse a painting of King David, dated 1779. Of particular interest is the wall tablet to Thomas Leake, who died in 1598. Around the edge

are hounds, stags, bows and hunting horns, since he was a Ranger of Sherwood Forest. Will Scarlet, one of Robin Hood's men, is said to be buried in the churchyard.

Blidworth Bottoms, page 53; **Haywood Oaks**, page 54.

In the locality: Burntstump Country Park, page 47; Robin Hood Way, page 54; Longdale Craft Centre, page 92; Papplewick Pumping Station, page 101; Abbeydale Farm Centre, page 104; Butterflies Pleasure Park, page 104; White Post Modern Farm Centre, page 106.

Blyth

The village takes its name from the nearby river, Blyth being the old name for the river Ryton. Its importance initially was probably due to the priory (page 63), but in 1194 a site just north, towards Styrrup, was one of five licensed as a tournament ground by Richard I. There were two leper hospitals at Blyth; one, St Edmund, has long since disappeared, but that of St John the Evangelist survives at the southern end of the long green in the High Street. Founded in 1226 by William Cressy of Hodsock, it was rebuilt in 1446, though the doorway, with its dogtooth ornament, seems to have been reused from an earlier building.

It was used in later years as a hostel for strangers and pregnant women, became a school in the seventeenth century and is now a house. The Hall has been demolished but the stable block and bridge over the Ryton, built by Carr in 1770, remain. Also late eighteenth-century is the old rectory on Church Green, with its cupola and Gothick windows. Smaller cottages opposite and others in the High Street have similar architectural features.

Church of St Mary and St Martin, page 63.

In the locality: Daneshill Lakes, page 47; Langold Country Park, page 49; Hodsock Priory Gardens, page 78.

Bothamsall
Bothamsall Castle, page 56.

Brinsley
Brinsley headstocks, page 97.

Bulwell
Seller's Wood, page 53.

Bunny
The present appearance of the village owes much to Sir Thomas Parkyns (1663-1741), who designed the Hall, the vicarage, a school and almshouses. The Hall was the last of these to be built, about 1720, and its most unusual feature is the tower, presumably erected as a belvedere. In the semicircular gable is a large stone carving of his coat of arms, in between two solid but unnecessary buttresses. The whole ungainly building, of red and black patterned brick with stone dressings and Ionic columns at the corners, displays a fertile imagination run riot. The southern façade is a later addition. The vicarage has been altered over the years but the school and almshouses of 1700 are little changed. They are in a more domestic style, three storeys, brick with stone quoins and again a large coat of arms. Among the Latin inscriptions above the ground-floor doors and windows is: *Scientia non habet inimicum nisi ignorantem* ('Learning has no enemy except ignorance'). Sir Thomas prided himself on his learning and wrote a Latin grammar! His

magnum opus, however, was *The Inn Play, or Cornish-Hugg Wrestler.* Wrestling was his passion, and he founded an annual wrestling match at Bunny that was held for 98 years. And so he appears on his memorial in the church lifesize and ready for a bout. A smaller carving depicts him on a rush mat, defeated by Father Time. Other members of the Parkyns family are commemorated: Richard, died 1603, and his wife face each other, with their children either side; Dame Anne, died 1725, mother of Sir Thomas, is depicted kneeling. The church itself, dedicated to St Mary, is mainly fourteenth-century, with a high crocketed spire. Work on the chancel was interrupted by the Black Death, which is why the upper part is in a later style than the lower. The east window was replaced when Sir Thomas reroofed the chancel. He may also have altered the gable of the south porch, the rest of it being fifteenth-century.

Bunny Old Wood West, page 51.

In the locality: Ruddington Framework Knitters Museum, page 94; Ruddington Village Museum, page 95.

Calverton
Painters' Paradise, page 83; Calverton framework knitters' cottages, page 97.

In the locality: Burntstump Country Park, page 47; Fox Wood hillfort, page 58; Oldox Camp, page 60; Playworld, page 105.

Car Colston
With not one but two village greens, this is one of the most attractive villages in the county. In the middle ages there were formerly houses on the greens and traces of these can still be seen, but they became common land at the enclosure of 1598, and so they remain, with grazing rights for cattle. There are several substantial houses: the Hall, built in an Elizabethan style in 1838 for the squarson, the Reverend John Girardot; Beech Close, dated 1719, with a pretty shell pediment over the front door; Brunsell Hall, one wing of an H-plan brick manor house of 1662; and Old Hall Farm. The last is not so important in itself, though it dates from 1812, but it stands on the site of the home of the village's most famous resident, Robert Thoroton

(1623-78). His invaluable book, *Antiquities of Nottinghamshire*, was published in 1677 and, updated by John Throsby at the end of the eighteenth century, remains a prime source for local historians. His desire that his bones might be left in peace was not heeded and his empty stone coffin stands in the church, St Mary. This is a mainly fourteenth-century building, though the lower stage of the tower dates from the previous century. The chancel is particularly fine, being higher than the nave, with large windows of curvilinear tracery. It is as decorative inside, with a notable piscina and sedilia. There is an interesting variety of woodwork: some fourteenth-century bench ends, a sixteenth-century pillar almsbox, a Jacobean pulpit and altar rails of 1732.

Carlton in Lindrick
Church of St John the Evangelist, page 63; Carlton Mill, page 98.

Carlton-on-Trent
Carlton is typical of many of the villages along the Trent in this part of the county, having a big house, a church and pleasant but unspectacular eighteenth-century houses. The

The forge at Carlton-on-Trent.

church, St Mary, was built in 1851, with only the south doorway reused from an earlier building. The architect was G. G. Place of Nottingham, who was responsible for building several churches in the county and restoring others. Here he let himself go with a tower, rather too thin, surmounted by pinnacles and a spire with peculiar plain square projections. Inside, he retained the curious cup-shaped font, altar table and two chests — all seventeenth-century. The Hall, which is open by appointment (telephone: 0636 821421), was built by Joseph Pocklington, a Newark banker, for himself in 1765. It is a handsome Georgian brick house, quite substantial, with a particularly fine staircase and good plasterwork, especially on the walls and ceiling of the dining room. The stable block is thought to be by Carr of York. The Great North Road, since bypassed by the A1, runs through the village, hence the importance of what was the Bell Inn, now Park Farmhouse, which has a large dining room, with Venetian windows, and the Old Forge, with a brick horseshoe around the entrance. There are some quite prosperous eighteenth-century brick houses with pantile roofs, and some smaller Victorian cottages, with ornate bargeboards. A seven-storey windmill stands just north of the village.

In the locality: Ossington church, page 68; Museum of Dolls and Bygone Childhood, page 85.

Chilwell
Chilwell Meadow, page 51.

Cinderhill
Quarry Holes Plantation, page 52.

Clarborough
Clarborough Tunnel, page 51.

Clifton
Although swamped by modern development, including a tower block, the old village of Clifton, to the west of the A453, retains much of its character. On the village green is the early eighteenth-century brick dovecote, the largest in the county, 38 by 18 feet (11.5 by 5.5 metres), with 2300 nesting boxes. Nearby

The stone in the wall of North Collingham churchyard, recording the flood level in 1795.

are the George Wells Almshouses, founded in 1709, with gazebos at the front corners of the garden. In Village Road are several thatched and timber-framed cottages, one of which has a datestone, 1707, but incorporates a fourteenth-century hall. At the end of the road are the church and the Hall, now part of Nottingham Trent University. Until 1953 this was the home of the Clifton family, who had held the manor since the thirteenth century. Although parts of it date from the seventeenth century, if not earlier, it was extensively re-modelled by Carr of York in the late eighteenth century. Large, but not showy, it is built of red brick with a Doric colonnade linking the wings. Alongside the river Trent is Clifton Grove, where Paul Morel and Clare Dawes strolled in Lawrence's *Sons and Lovers*.

Brecks Plantation and Glapton Wood, page 51; **Fairham Brook**, page 52; **church of St Mary**, page 63.

In the locality: Barton in Fabis dovecote, page 56; Ruddington Framework Knitters Museum, page 94; Ruddington Village Museum, page 95; Wilford Bridge tollhouse, page 103.

Clipstone

Clipstone Forest, page 53; King John's Palace, page 58.

Clumber

Clumber Park, page 47; church of St Mary the Virgin, page 64.

Coddington

It was from Coddington that Prince Rupert led the charge which routed Parliament's forces when Newark was besieged in 1644, and traces of Civil War earthworks remain around the village. There is much pleasant red brick housing here, notably Old Manor Farm of 1714, and a decaying four-storey tarred brick windmill built around 1859. The church, All Saints, is thirteenth-century but was drastically restored by Bodley in 1864. However, no expense was spared; the chancel ceiling is richly painted and there is fine woodwork in the choirstalls, sedilia and screen. Best of all is the stained glass by Morris, Burne-Jones and Ford Madox Brown.

Collingham

North and South Collingham, which have become one village, lie along the old course of the river Trent, now called the Fleet. The Trent changed its course to run over a mile to the west of the village in about 1600. Nonetheless, the village was under 5 feet (1.5 metres) of water in the flooding of 1795, as a stone in the wall of North Collingham churchyard records. The church, All Saints, is mainly thirteenth-century, with a notable fifteenth-century north porch. Inside are seven misericords, with coats of arms and strange beasts, that were put above the chancel arch when the choirstalls were destroyed in the nineteenth century. The double piscina by the chancel arch suggests that there was an altar on the rood screen as well as those in the sanctuary and side chapels, each with a single piscina. The simple thirteenth-century font has a cover which looks Jacobean. At the northern end of the village is the stump of the fourteenth-century village cross.

The church of St John Baptist, South Collingham, has a much taller tower than its neighbour. This is thirteenth century, as is the south aisle. The north arcade, however, is Norman, with zigzag ornament and a curious carving of a grotesque beast with a man's head in its jaws. In contrast, the fine rood screen was erected as recently as 1940. There are many interesting houses here. The Nunnery in South End is sixteenth- or early seventeenth-century and there are a number of good Georgian buildings in Low Street and High Street, where there is also a single-storey cottage with a pyramidal thatched roof. The Old Hall in Low Street is believed to be the birthplace of John Blow (1648-1708), the composer and teacher of Henry Purcell.

In the locality: Spalford Warren, page 53; Trent Valley Way, page 55; Holme by Newark church, page 66.

Colwick
Colwick Country Park, page 47.

Cromwell
Vina Cooke Museum of Dolls and Bygone Childhood, page 85.

Cuckney
Cuckney Castle, page 58.

Darlton
Kingshaugh, page 58.

Daybrook
Morleys' hosiery factory, page 98.

East Leake
Although considerably extended in recent years, East Leake still retains a village heart, with a stream flowing beside its little green and a few seventeenth- and eighteenth-century brick houses. Its most unusual feature is a vamping horn, similar to that at South Scarle and one of only nine in England. It is 7 feet 9

inches (2.4 metres) long and trumpet-shaped. It was used until 1855 by one of the choirmen to drone out the bass of the hymn tunes. It is to be seen in the church, St Mary. The north wall of the nave is Norman, as evidenced by the herringbone masonry and small high windows, and the tower is slightly later. In the fifteenth century a spire was added and the nave given a clerestory.

In the locality: Bunny Old Wood, page 51.

East Markham
The medieval village stood south of the church, as indicated not only by earthworks but by the fact that the church porch faces south, away from the present village. It was after a serious outbreak of the plague in 1609, when 115 people died, that it was rebuilt to the north, nearer the Lincoln road. The manor house to the west of the church is seventeenth-century, built of brick with a roof of pantiles, and the other big house, Markham Hall, was built in a classical style in 1777. There is a variety of interesting brickwork in the smaller houses and in Plantation Road stand two of the village's four dovecotes and the pinfold or pound. About 1$\frac{1}{2}$ miles (2.5 km) to the west is Cleveland Mill, a four-storey brick tower mill built in 1837.

Church of St John the Baptist, page 64.

In the locality: Eaton Wood, page 52; Kingshaugh, page 58; Longbottoms Mill, page 98.

Eastwood
D.H.Lawrence Birthplace Museum, page 85: Shipley Lock aqueduct, page 102.

Edwinstowe
The name means 'the holy place of Edwin', and it seems likely that the body of King Edwin was brought here after the battle of Heathfield in 633. Certainly there was a chapel dedicated to him, as a Christian martyr, in the middle ages, between Edwinstowe and Warsop. The church, however, is dedicated to St Mary. The tower is of the twelfth century, with a nineteenth-century spire, perhaps based on that rebuilt after a storm in 1680. The nave and chancel are slightly later than the tower, with a fifteenth-century

clerestory and battlements. Dr E. C. Brewer, famous for his *Dictionary of Phrase and Fable*, lies buried in the churchyard. Although Robin Hood merits a long entry in this massive tome, Brewer does not mention the local legend that Robin and Maid Marian were married here by Friar Tuck.

Sherwood Forest Country Park, page 50; **Sherwood Forest Amusement Park**, page 105; **Sherwood Forest Farm Park**, page 105.

In the locality: Rufford Country Park, page 49; Clipstone Forest, page 53; Little John Challenge Walk, page 54; Robin Hood Way, page 54; King John's Palace, page 58; Rufford Abbey, page 61; Ollerton watermill, page 101.

Egmanton

Egmanton Castle, page 58; church of St Mary, page 64.

Epperstone

Although none of its buildings is of exceptional architectural interest, this is a particularly pleasant and unspoilt village, with trees along the main street and a variety of Victorian, Georgian and earlier houses. Its rural nature is emphasised by the pinfold or pound for stray cattle and several dovecotes, notably one of 1700 belonging to the Manor and another opposite the Cross Keys. The church, Holy Cross, is largely thirteenth-century, with a later spire.

Farnsfield

Farnsfield to Southwell Trail, page 53; Butterflies Pleasure Park, page 104; White Post Modern Farm Centre, page 106.

Fiskerton

Fiskerton Mill, page 98.

Fledborough

Church of St Gregory, page 64.

Gedling

Church of All Hallows, page 66.

Gonalston

Like Epperstone, this is another pretty village near the Dover Beck that flows into the Trent.

T. C. Hine was the architect who carried out the Victorianisation of Gonalston Hall in 1851, and in 1853 he turned his attention to the church, St Lawrence. Although the exterior appears to be almost entirely of this date, particularly the tower and spire, the chancel is old and, whereas it is not unusual to go up steps into the chancel, here one goes down three steps. There are three early fourteenth-century monuments to members of the de Heriz family, of which that to Matilda is the best preserved. The stone altar slab on which the communion table now stands was brought here from the demolished Spital of St Mary Magdalen, formerly on the road to Thurgarton. The altar rails are seventeenth-century and the royal arms and pulpit eighteenth-century. In the village is a forge dated 1845, with a horseshoe arch in the brickwork, similar to that at Carlton-on-Trent (page 16).

Edwinstowe church, where Robin Hood is said to have married Maid Marian.

Kelham Hall in 1890.

To the south, on the Lowdham to Thurgarton road, stands Cliff Mill. It is now a private residence but was built in the late eighteenth century as a cotton mill, with the Dover Beck driving the 15 foot (4.5 metre) diameter waterwheel. The brutal treatment of the young apprentices who worked there was graphically described in the 'Memoir of Robert Blincoe, an orphan boy, sent from the workhouse of St Pancras, London, at seven years of age to endure the horrors of a cotton mill, through his infancy and youth, with a minute detail of his sufferings', published by John Brown in 1832.

In the locality: Bleasby dovecote, page 56; Thurgarton Priory, page 74.

Greasley
Greasley Castle, page 58.

Gringley on the Hill
Built along a ridge, this village offers commanding views over all the surrounding countryside. It may be only 82 feet (25 metres) above sea level but one can see far into Yorkshire to the north and west, into Lincolnshire to the east and into the rest of Nottingham-shire stretching into the distance southwards. Beacon Hill, on the eastern outskirts, is the best vantage point and may have been the site of a prehistoric settlement. The church, St Peter and St Paul, has a blocked Norman doorway in the tower, proclaiming its antiquity, though the upper storeys are fifteenth-century. The north aisle dates from the first half of the thirteenth century but was restored in the early eighteenth, which accounts for the classical north doorway. The elegant pillar piscina in the chancel is unusual and also thirteenth-century. North-west of the church stands the column of a medieval cross, prominent at the centre of the community. Close by is one of the three dovecotes belonging to the more prosperous buildings of the village. Further west is a four-storey brick windmill with only the struts of its cap left.

In the locality: Trent Valley Way, page 55; Mattersey Priory, page 59.

Halam
Just west of Southwell, Halam is a quiet village of red brick and pantiles, farmhouses and dovecotes. The church, St Michael, is Norman with a low broad tower and a notable

chancel arch. The tower arch and south arcade are thirteenth-century. Its finest feature is probably the stained glass: four fourteenth-century figures of St Christopher carrying Christ, St Blaise, Adam delving and Eve spinning. This is complemented by five early twentieth-century windows, mainly designed by Burne-Jones and made by Morris & Company. To the north of the village, towards Kirklington, is an eighteenth-century watermill.

In the locality: Southwell Minster, page 70; Norwood Park, page 81; Bramley Apple Display, page 104.

Haughton
The World of Robin Hood, page 106.

Hawksworth
Unfairly neglected by the majority of guidebooks, this is one of a number of attractive villages in the Vale of Belvoir. The church is much older than might be thought at first glance. While the base of the tower is thirteenth-century, of stone, the upper storey is seventeenth-century brick and the rest of the church is nineteenth-century. However, built into the south wall of the tower is a Norman tympanum with a central cross flanked by two figures, possibly the crucified thieves, and two roundels of the Agnus Dei and an angel. The Latin inscription states that 'Walter and his wife Cecelina caused this church to be built in honour of our Lord and St Mary the Virgin and of all the saints of God at the same time'. Inside the tower is part of a Saxon cross shaft with crosses and interlace decoration. The stone Manor House is sixteenth-century with a dovecote of 1665. Forming the northern boundary of the parish is Long Hedge Lane, an ancient trackway which runs from Bottesford to Hazelford ferry on the river Trent.

In the locality: Sibthorpe dovecote, page 62; Thoroton dovecote, page 62.

Hawton
Church of All Saints, page 66.

Hodsock
Hodsock Priory Gardens, page 78.

Holme by Newark
Church of St Giles, page 66.

Holme Pierrepont
Holme Pierrepont Country Park, page 49; Holme Pierrepont Hall, page 78.

Kelham
It was at Kelham that Charles I spent his first night of captivity after surrendering to the Scots at Southwell on 5th May 1646. The Hall burnt down at the end of the seventeenth century and was rebuilt some thirty years later, but this house in its turn was almost entirely destroyed by fire in 1857. So it was that George Gilbert Scott, who was carrying out alterations at the time, was entrusted with the task of rebuilding it of red brick and stone in his best railway-station style. Its deliberately irregular layout with three different towers makes for an interesting skyline but gives an impression of striving for novelty for its own sake, especially in the variety of window designs. Early in the twentieth century it became the home of the Society of the Sacred Mission, an Anglican religious community, who used it as a theological college. It was for them that the Byzantine chapel was built, now stripped of its grandeur since the Hall was taken over as offices by the newly formed District Council in 1973. The church, St Wilfrid, lies to the south of the Hall. It is mainly fifteenth-century, but with an eighteenth-century mausoleum attached to house the tomb of Robert Sutton, Lord Lexington (died 1723), and his wife, whose splendid effigies recline, facing away from each other, on a mattress. Inside, the fifteenth-century screens are particularly fine.

Kingston on Soar
This is a pleasant estate village of mainly Victorian brick cottages around a triangular green. The nave, aisle and tower of the church, St Wilfrid, were rebuilt in 1900 but the chancel and its aisle are dated 1538. In about 1540 the Babington chantry was built. The tomb chest has gone but the amazing canopy on its four columns still remains. This is covered in carvings: many little figures and notably babes in tuns, a pun on the name of Babington. The

canopy is vaulted, with battlements and pinnacles above, and there is a relief of the Last Judgement against the east wall.

In the locality: Ratcliffe on Soar church, page 70.

Kirton
Kirton Wood, page 52.

Lambley
Playworld, page 105.

Langar
Church of St Andrew, page 66; Wild Flower Farm Visitors Centre, page 106.

Langold
Langold Country Park, page 49.

Laxton
For a variety of reasons Laxton is a fascinating village. Its prime claim to fame is that it is the only village to retain its medieval strip-farming system. Three of the medieval open

Laxton church with its elaborate clerestory.

fields have never been enclosed and even now the Court Leet meets every 23rd November to administer the annual leases of West Field, South Field and Mill Field, 483 acres (195 hectares) in all. This is why the farmhouses and outbuildings, which are mainly eighteenth-century, are in the village rather than some distance outside. The Court Leet also appoints a pinder to impound stray animals in the pinfold, next to the Dovecote inn. A Laxton Trail leads around the village and its back lane, and a Visitor Centre gives more information.

Laxton is also noted for its motte and bailey castle, built soon after the Norman conquest, and one of the best preserved in the county. The church, St Michael, is thirteenth-century with a fourteenth-century chancel. The nave was given a lavish clerestory and the top stage of the tower was added at the end of the fifteenth century. In a restoration of 1860 the nave was shortened and the tower entirely rebuilt and given a pyramidal roof. Inside the chancel are an Easter sepulchre and sedilia; both the chancel screen and that in the north aisle, dated 1532, are much restored. There are a number of monumental effigies, but in poor condition. The figure of the second wife of Adam de Everingham (died 1341) is unusual in being the only wooden one in Nottinghamshire.

Laxton Visitor Centre, page 85.

In the locality: Kirton Wood, page 52; Egmanton Castle, page 58; churches at Egmanton, page 64; and Ossington, page 68.

Linby
Newstead Abbey, page 78; Castle Mill, page 98.

Littleborough
To look at this hamlet now, one would not guess at its former importance at the crossing of the Trent on the Till Bridge Lane from Lincoln to Doncaster. It was known to the Romans as *Segelocum* and a number of archaeological finds have been made, including in 1860 a Roman stone coffin containing the body of a young woman, which disintegrated on opening. Some Roman tiles were built into the herringbone masonry of

the tiny Norman church, only 45 feet long by 15 feet wide (13.5 by 4.5 metres). It has hardly been altered since it was built: even one of the bells in the bellcote dates from about 1200 and the other from about 1350. This is one of the remotest spots in the county.

Littleborough Toll Cottage, page 98.

Mansfield

Early closing, Wednesday; market days, Monday, Thursday, Friday and Saturday.

Celia Fiennes wrote in the seventeenth century: 'There is nothing remarkable here.' The construction of the ring road and shopping precinct has taken its toll of some of the older buildings, and the railway viaduct of 1875, which straddles the town centre, can hardly be called picturesque, but the town is not as drab as one might fear. The tower of the parish church, St Peter and St Paul, is Norman, with a top stage added about 1300, when the interior was remodelled. Its spire was not erected until late in the seventeenth century. The chancel and side chapels are largely fifteenth-century. In the chancel and in both porches are foliate cross slabs, and in the south chapel is an incised slab to a priest. Immediately south of the church is the Old Grammar School, founded in the reign of Queen Elizabeth I, rebuilt in 1714-19, restored and enlarged in 1851. Just north of the church is a fine late seventeenth-century house. The two Victorian churches, St John the Evangelist and St Mark, are both good examples of the period.

Mansfield was noted for its nonconformist leanings in the seventeenth century and the Old Parsonage, which dates from this time, is where one such congregation met. In 1702 they built the Old Meeting House, just behind it. Although it was altered in the nineteenth century and excellent stained glass by Morris & Company was inserted early in the twentieth, it still retains some of its original atmosphere — and is one of the oldest chapels still in use in the county.

The Market Place is still the focal point of the town, with T. C. Hine's Gothic monument to Lord George Bentinck, who died in 1848, as its centrepiece. An earlier benefactor, Lady Oxford, built the Moot Hall in 1752, which

bears her coat of arms. It is plainer and more pleasing than the rather serious neo-classical Town Hall of 1836. The sixteenth- or seventeenth-century Market Cross, however, is in Westgate. Notice, nearby, Waverley House, built in 1754 in a patchwork of different styles.

Museum and Art Gallery, page 85; **Kings Mill viaduct**, page 98.

In the locality: Sherwood Forest Country Park, page 50; Spa Ponds, page 53; Blidworth Bottoms, page 53; Clipstone Forest, page 53; Haywood Oaks, page 54; Meden Trail, page 54; Thieves Wood and Harlow Wood, page 54; King John's Palace, page 58; Teversal church, page 72; Newstead Abbey, page 78; Longdale Craft Centre, page 92; Abbeydale Farm Centre, page 104; Sherwood Forest Amusement Park, page 105; Sherwood Forest Farm Park, page 105.

Mansfield Woodhouse

Meden Trail, page 54.

Mattersey

Mattersey Priory, page 59.

Newark

Early closing, Thursday; market days, Monday, Wednesday, Friday and Saturday.

Newark is noted not only for its parish church and castle, but for its market place and variety of architecture. The town owed its prosperity to the major transport links of the Trent, the Fosse Way and the Great North Road and was a centre for agriculture, particularly wool in the middle ages, and a coaching stop in the eighteenth and nineteenth centuries. Because of its decline in the twentieth century it is comparatively unspoilt and its buildings are gradually being restored. The Market Place has benefited from this. Its oldest building is the former White Hart inn, with its timber-framed upper storeys and little figures of saints. The exterior dates from the late fifteenth century, but the interior is over a century older. Also on the south side are the old Saracen's Head inn, with an appropriate bust in a niche on the façade, and the Clinton Arms, both early eighteenth-century with colonnades at street level. Sir Walter Scott patronised the former whereas Byron and

Gladstone, who was Member of Parliament for Newark from 1832 to 1845, preferred the latter. The west side is dominated by the Town Hall, built *c*.1775 by Carr of York. It is a magnificent piece of civic architecture in the classical style, with a central colonnade and portico, surmounted by a figure of Justice. In the north-eastern corner is a distinguished Queen Anne house with a splendid doorway. It was in this building that Byron's first poetry was published. The actual printing press is in the Newark Museum. On the opposite corner is the late Victorian National Westminster Bank, which stands on the site of Hercules Clay's house. Alderman Clay had several vivid dreams during the siege of Newark that his house would receive a direct hit. He moved his family out not long before his presentiment became a reality.

Nearby, in Stodman Street, is the sixteenth-century timber-framed Governor's House, so called because it was the residence of the Governor during the Civil War. Further along is another timber-framed building, dated to 1489, the Woolpack inn. At the end of Stodman Street, in Castlegate, is the mid nineteenth-century Corn Exchange, in Italian baroque style, testament to Newark's agricultural trade. Most of the other buildings in Castlegate are eighteenth-century town houses. At the junction with Beast Market is the Ossington Coffee Palace, built in 1882 to a design by Ernest George & Peto for Viscountess Ossington, who had 'an earnest desire to promote the cause of temperance'. This was outweighed by the desire of travellers for stronger refreshment, and the building has had a variety of uses since then. On the other side of the road is Kirkgate, with not only a fine view of the church spire, but also a number of interesting buildings ranging from a sixteenth-century timber-framed house to the former Nottingham and Notts Bank of 1887 by Watson Fothergill in a flamboyant Italian Gothic style, which is now a school of violin making.

North of Castlegate is Northgate, worth exploring for its seventeenth- and eighteenth-century houses and its brewing connections. Number 35 is a complex of eighteenth-century housing, maltings and a kiln around a court-yard. On the same side of the road is the Warwicks & Richardson (now John Smith) brewery built of red brick in 1882-90 in Queen Anne style, with maltings of 1864 and bottling store of 1920 lying back from the road. Some of the larger maltings nearby have been demolished, but the Peach building still stands. At the southern end of the town centre in Albert Street is another fine brewery building, the former Castle Brewery offices, also belonging to John Smith. This too was built in 1882, but in grey stone and in French Renaissance *château* style, with a central clock-tower, and a frieze of Newark Castle. A stroll along Millgate or Appletongate is rewarding, not just for the museums, but for a different perspective on the town a trip along the river on a boat is recommended (the Lock and Castle Line; telephone: 0636 707939).

Newark Castle, page 60; **Queen's Sconce**, page 60; **church of St Mary Magdalen**, page 67; **Millgate Folk Museum**, page 86; **Newark Air Museum**, page 86; **Newark Civic Plate Collection**, page 86; **Newark Museum**, page 86.

In the locality: Trent Valley Way, page 55; Barnby in the Willows dovecote, page 56; Sibthorpe dovecote, page 62; churches at Fledborough, page 64; Hawton, page 66; Holme by Newark, page 66; and Ossington, page 68; Southwell Minster, page 70; Museum of Dolls and Bygone Childhood, page 85; British Horological Institute, page 95; Fiskerton Mill, page 98; Reg Taylor's Swan Sanctuary, page 105.

New Clipstone
Spa Ponds, page 53.

Normanton
Reg Taylor's Swan Sanctuary, page 105.

North Clifton
Pureland Japanese Garden, page 84.

North Leverton
North Leverton windmill, page 99.

Norwell
This little village, whose name is a contraction of Northwell (as opposed to Southwell),

was once prosperous with a fair and weekly market. The moated sites of five manor houses still survive, three of which were prebends of Southwell Minster. The most obvious is south of the church (Norwell Overhall); another is on the west side of the main street in the middle of the village (Norwell Tertia Pars) and south of the village is Norwell Pallishall. The fourth is on the road to Carlton-on-Trent and the last at Norwell Woodhouse. The church, St Laurence, is quite large for the present size of the village. The lower stages of the tower are thirteenth-century, as are the chancel, chancel arch with rood stairs and south aisle. The north aisle and transept date from the fourteenth century and the top stage of the tower, with pinnacles, gargoyles and battlements, from the fifteenth. The clerestory is slightly later. Both transepts have aumbries, one combined with a piscina. There is an effigy to an unknown lady, early fourteenth-century, which is still in very good condition, and another, of a knight, possibly Sir John di Lisure (died 1330). Two of the stained glass windows are by Kempe.

The village itself is quite attractive with a number of seventeenth- and eighteenth-century houses and a Wesleyan chapel of 1843. A four-storey windmill of 1852, built of brick and tarred, stands not far from the church, but without cap or sails. Many villages in the county still have a pinfold, or pound, but Norwell's is unusual in being circular and built of brick, dating from the late eighteenth or early nineteenth century. It stands at the corner of the main street and the road to Bathley.

In the locality: Ossington church, page 68; Museum of Dolls and Bygone Childhood, page 85.

Nottingham
Early closing, Thursday; market days, Monday to Saturday.
Nottingham with all its suburbs now has a population of around 280,000. Bronze age axes and spearheads discovered here provide the earliest evidence of settlement and excavations in the Lace Market have revealed iron age grain-storage pits. A Roman crematorium was found at the Castle but then there

The spire of Newark church seen from Kirkgate in the 1930s.

is no further trace of human occupation until Saxon times. The first reference to *Snotenga-ham* is in the Anglo-Saxon Chronicle of 867, though Snot must have founded it at least three centuries earlier. The Saxon settlement was around St Mary's, and the Norman town lay beneath the castle walls. The two gradually merged and the town became prosperous. Its medieval trades gave their names to its streets (frequently called 'gate' from the Norse *gata,*a street): Barker Gate for the tanners, Fletcher Gate for the butchers (flesh-hewers), Lister Gate for the dyers, Pilcher Gate for the furriers and Fisher Gate for the fishmongers. Sharp practice was rife. The Mayor was fined in 1512 for overcharging customers by selling five herrings for a penny instead of seven and the fact that the silver-smith Nicholas Gorson was fined for selling substandard goods in 1542 and 1543 did not

The Council House, Nottingham.

prevent him being made Sheriff in 1550. In the following centuries travellers were unanimous in their praise of Nottingham and its beer. Celia Fiennes, writing in 1697, thought it 'the neatest town I have seen' and drank 'the strongest and best Nottingham ale that looked very pale but exceeding clear'. Daniel Defoe concurred, calling it 'one of the most beautiful and pleasant towns in England', and noting that 'they brew a very good liquor here'. In 1675 Thomas Baskerville said: 'Here is Paradise restored.' Modern visitors can make up their own minds as to whether or not they can endorse these comments.

Although there has been no market in the **Old Market Square** since 1928 and trade has shifted to the Victoria and Broadmarsh shopping centres, it is still thought of as the hub of the city. It is almost 6 acres (2.5 hectares) in area and the architecture is mostly of the nineteenth and twentieth centuries. Three older survivals are the former **Flying Horse hotel**, said to date back to 1483, though much restored since then, which stands in Poultry, just south of the Council House; the **Bell Inn** in Angel Row, whose interior is partly medieval, even if the exterior is of about 1830; and **Bromley House** of 1752. The square is dominated by the **Council House**, designed by the Nottingham architect Cecil Howitt. Built in 1927-9, it has a Greek portico and central dome and is guarded by two lions. Inside is the **Exchange Arcade** with a variety of shops and a good view of the interior of the dome. Three nineteenth-century buildings are worthy of note: **Yates Wine Lodge**, an extravagant gin palace of 1876; the **National Westminster Bank** (formerly Smith's) in the style of an Italian palazzo, 1878; and Watson Fothergill's 1897 **Queen's Chambers**, in a quirky Tudor style, at the corner of King Street. Since it was the year of Victoria's Diamond Jubilee her head is carved on the side, with a definite 'we are not amused' expression. At the angle of King Street and Queen Street is the **Prudential Building** of 1892, in the same style as the company's famous London offices.

The Old Market Square is a good starting point for a walk around the city, which has been devised as a figure of eight to make one

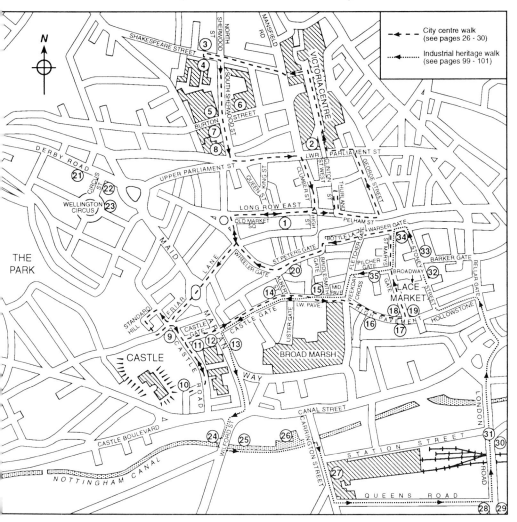

Map of Nottingham city centre. Key: 1 Council House and tourist information office; 2 Victoria Centre; 3 Synagogue; 4 Nottingham Trent University; 5 Newton Building; 6 Guildhall; 7 Royal Concert Hall; 8 Theatre Royal; 9 Castle Gatehouse: 10 Brewhouse Yard Museum; 11 Severns Building (The Lace Centre); 12 Museum of Costume and Textiles; 13 Church of St Nicholas; 14 Congregational Centre; 15 Post Office; 16 Story of Nottingham Lace; 17 Shire Hall; 18 County House; 19 Church of St Mary; 20 Church of St Peter; 21 Roman Catholic Cathedral of St Barnabas; 22 Albert Hall; 23 Nottingham Playhouse; 24 Castle Lock; 25 British Waterways Board warehouse; 26 Canal Museum; 27 Midland Station; 28 Hicking Pentecost building; 29 Eastcroft Depot; 30 London Road Station; 31 Station Street Bridge; 32 Mills Building; 33 Barker Gate House; 34 Adams & Page warehouse: 35 Warehouses in Pilcher Gate.

Caves hollowed out of the rock below Nottingham Castle.

long or two shorter tours. Leave the Market Square along Long Row East. At the junction with High Street is the former **Boots Store**, built in 1904 by Jesse Boot as his flagship and one of the first in the city to have electric light. In buff terracotta with Art Nouveau windows, it has a cupola at one corner and cherubs holding a shield with the initial B at the other. Continue along Pelham Street and turn left along Thurland Street. On the left is another of Watson Fothergill's exuberant designs that enliven Nottingham. This is the **Nottingham and Notts Bank** of 1882 in Early English style with fine stone carvings, including a chained monkey, representing the burden of a mortgage, on one of the capitals inside. On the other side of the road is the more restrained **Corn Exchange** by T. C. Hine in his 'Anglo-Italian' style of 1850. Retrace your steps and walk up Pelham Street past the splendid **Thurland Hall**, a late Victorian pub. On the right stands **Journal Chambers**, 1860, in multicoloured brick, where J. M. Barrie, author of *Peter Pan,* worked for the *Nottingham Journal* in 1883-4. Turn left into George Street. On the right is the former **Roman Catholic chapel** of 1828

with stone façade, classical pediment and Gothic windows. On the left are **Watson Fothergill's former offices**, built in 1895. (There is sometimes confusion over his name because he changed it by deed poll in 1892 from Fothergill Watson to Watson Fothergill.) They are built in a combination of his favourite styles and materials, Gothic brick and stone with half-timbering on the top storey. The decoration includes a statue of a medieval architect — perhaps how he saw himself — four terracotta panels showing several buildings in construction, and busts of his heroes, Pugin and Street. This last was probably an intentional joke — a bust of George Edmund Street in George Street. Turn left at Lower Parliament Street. On the corner is the **Methodist Church** of 1874 by R. C. Sutton, with a modern extension. Further along, on the corner of Clinton Street West is another of Watson Fothergill's buildings, the 1896 shop for **Furley & Company**. It has four fine terracotta panels. On the other side of Lower Parliament Street is the **Victoria Centre**, built on the site of Victoria Station in 1972. It is worth going in to see Rowland Emmett's **Time Fountain** with various woodland creatures constantly turning on a Heath Robinson sort of mechanism. Walk further on into the centre and then turn left to emerge in Mansfield Road by the **Clock Tower**, which is all that remains of Lambert's 1901 station building. Cross Mansfield Road then look up the hill for Watson Fothergill's 1899 pub, the **City Alehouse**, on the right. Walk along Shakespeare Street across North and South Sherwood Street. On the right is the **Synagogue**, originally an 1854 Wesleyan Reform chapel, and past that the Victorian Gothic **Registrar's Office**, once the offices of the guardians of the Poor Law. Opposite is the **Nottingham Trent University**, a High Gothic building that originated in 1881 as University College, becoming a technical college in 1945 when Nottingham University moved the last of its departments out to its present campus, and finally, after a series of changes of name, coming full circle to university status again. Go back down Shakespeare Street and turn right down South Sherwood Street. On the right is the **Newton Building** of 1956-8 by Cecil Howitt, who designed not only the Council House and several buildings for Nottingham University but also Staythorpe power station, to which the Newton Building bears a certain resemblance. On the left is the **Guildhall** of 1887-8 in French Renaissance style. Across Burton Street is the 1982 **Royal Concert Hall** and behind that the **Theatre Royal**, whose grand portico becomes visible only as one turns into Upper Parliament Street. This is all that survives of the 1865 theatre since the auditorium was sumptuously remodelled in 1897 and the foyer interior revamped in 1976-8. Go east along Upper Parliament Street. Across the road is the former **Elite Cinema**, completely covered in white tiles, some with Art Nouveau decoration, and statues in niches on the top storey. Further along are the **Express Chambers**, one of Watson Fothergill's early commissions, built in 1876 and extended in 1899. Its corner tower and carvings of mythical beasts betray the influence of another of his heroes, William Burges. Turn right down Clumber Street to rejoin the Market Square at Long Row East.

For the second leg, leave Market Square by

Friar Lane. Almost at the castle gates turn right up Standard Hill, then first left. It was here that Charles I raised the Royal Standard in 1642 at the beginning of the Civil War. Turn left down King Charles Street, down the steps and left again to the **Castle Gatehouse**. In the moat stands James Woodford's 1952 **statue of Robin Hood**. Opposite, the terrace of houses running down the hill, starting with the **Old Castle Inn**, is immediately recognisable as the work of the ubiquitous Fothergill Watson. Further down the hill, just below the castle walls, is the **Trip to Jerusalem** public house, said to date back to 1189, though the present buildings are seventeenth-century. Part of the interior, particularly the cellars, is cut into the rock. This is one of the few places in England where the pub game of Ringing the Bull is still played. Nearby is the **Brewhouse Yard Museum**. Back up the hill,

The Trip to Jerusalem in Nottingham is said to be the oldest inn in England.

on the corner of Castle Gate is **Severns**, the medieval building housing the Lace Centre. In Castle Gate is the **Museum of Costume and Textiles**. Opposite, on the corner of Maid Marian Way, is **Newdigate House**, built about 1680, with tasteful detail and excellent early eighteenth-century wrought ironwork. It was here that Marshal Tallard was held after his defeat at Blenheim in 1704. Across Maid Marian Way, a little further down, is **St Nicholas church**. The old church was destroyed by Colonel Hutchinson (page 113) in the Civil War, because the Royalists were using the tower as a gun emplacement when they besieged the castle. The new building, in brick, was started in 1671 and not completed until 1682. The aisles are both eighteenth-century additions. The inlaid pulpit was made in 1783 and the chancel panelling and communion rails are a century earlier. Continue east along Castle Gate. On the corner with St Nicholas Street is the **Royal Children**, where the publican once sold whale oil, used in oil lamps — hence the whale bone above the door. Next to it is the **Salutation Inn**, early sixteenth-century and timber-framed, though reputed to date back to 1240. Further along Castle Gate are some notable Georgian buildings, especially **numbers 32 to 36** and **number 19**, dated 1775, with a fine pedimented doorway and elaborate window above. With the **Congregational Centre**, a former chapel built in Italianate style in 1863 and now the national headquarters of the Congregational Federation, we move into a more Victorian quarter. The adjacent schoolrooms were built in a similar style twenty years later. On the corner of Lister Gate and Low Pavement is a former **warehouse** of 1854 by T. C. Hine, similar to those in the Lace Market, with several interesting late nineteenth- and early twentieth-century houses alongside on Low Pavement. Further along on the left is the **Post Office**, originally built as the Assembly Rooms, with an imposing façade of Corinthian columns. Of the same date, 1836, is the more severely classical **Nottingham Savings Bank,** designed by Thomas Hawksley, the city's water engineer. Back on the south side are more Georgian houses: **Enfield House** of about 1750, with its

magnificent Venetian windows; **Willoughby House**, built in 1738; and **numbers 24 and 26** of 1733, called Vault Halls, because they were built over the rock cellars which were used as the vaults of the Woolstaplers in the middle ages. Carry on along Middle Pavement to Weekday Cross, which was the Saxon market place, and across to High Pavement. Here is the former Unitarian chapel that houses the **Story of Nottingham Lace**. Further along is the **Shire Hall**, built in 1770 and remodelled after a fire in 1876 by T. C. Hine. On the other side of the road is the **County House**, built in about 1730 and extended in a heavy classical style in 1833 when it became the judges' lodgings. On the corner of St Mary's Gate stands **St Mary's church**. Carry on along St Mary's Gate and turn left in Warser Gate, across Fletcher Gate and down Bottle Lane to Bridlesmith Gate. Connoisseurs of Victorian pub architecture will enjoy the **Dog and Bear Hotel** with its lavish carving of 1876. The rather Italianate **County Court** in St Peter's Gate was built in 1875, and the former **Waterworks Office** (now Standard Chartered Bank) in Venetian Gothic a year earlier.

St Peter's church, like St Nicholas, was founded by the Normans in the 'French Borough', as opposed to St Mary's, which dates from Saxon times, in the 'English Borough'. The oldest part of the present church is the early thirteenth-century south arcade; the tower with its spire dates from about 1340 and the north arcade from about 1360. The roofs of the nave and south aisle are early sixteenth-century. Much damage, including the destruction of the chancel, was caused when the castle garrison retook the church from the Royalists in 1644. Hence the bowl of the font is late seventeenth-century on a fourteenth-century base. Although the chancel was rebuilt in 1670 a totally new chancel, together with the north transept, was built in 1875. There is some good Victorian and modern glass and a fine organ case of 1770. Outside the church, in Albert Street, is a modern sculpture by Paul Mason, called **Leaf Stem**. A walk along Wheeler Gate will lead back to the Market Square.

West and north-west of the Castle is **The**

Park. Originally royal hunting grounds, it was not developed for housing until 1827. It is of particular interest to aficionados of Victorian architecture and town planning. The houses are all shapes and sizes, many being by T. C. Hine and a few by Watson Fothergill. On the edge of The Park, on Derby Road, is **St Barnabas**, the Roman Catholic cathedral. Built in 1841 by Pugin in an Early English style, it is rather severe, but with a more fanciful spire. The interior has been reordered and all that remains of Pugin's original decoration is the crucifix and the stained glass windows in the aisles. Across North Circus Street is Nottingham's **Albert Hall,** built in 1907 by A. E. Lambert, the designer of the Midland and Victoria stations, in music-hall style with much buff terracotta. Alongside, on Wellington Circus, is the other major theatre, the **Nottingham Playhouse,** one of the more important modern contributions to the city's architecture.

Lenton Priory, page 59; **church of St Mary**, page 68; **Wollaton Hall**, page 84; **Castle and Castle Museum**, pages 81 and 90; **Brewhouse Yard Museum**, page 88; **Canal Museum**, page 88; **Greens Mill**, page 89; **Museum of Costume and Textiles**, page 89; **Natural History Museum**, page 90; **Industrial Museum**, page 91; **Sherwood Foresters Regimental Museum**, page 92; **Story of Nottingham Lace**, page 92; **industrial heritage**, page 99; **Wilford Bridge tollhouse**, page 103; **Lace Centre**, page 104; **Brass Rubbing Centre**, page 105; **Nottingham Story**, page 105; **Tales of Robin Hood**, page 105.

In the locality: Bestwood Country Park, page 47; Colwick Country Park, page 47; Holme Pierrepont Country Park and Hall, pages 49 and 78; Brecks Plantation and Glapton Wood, page 51; Fairham Brook, page 52; Harrison's Plantation and Martin's Pond, page 52; Oldmoor Wood, page 52; Quarry Holes Plantation, page 52; Seller's Wood, page 53; churches at Clifton, page 63; Gedling, page 66; Strelley, page 72; and Wollaton, page 75; Model Aviation Centre, page 85; Ruddington Framework Knitters' Museum and Village Museum, pages 94 and 95; Anglo-Scotian Mills, page 96; Bestwood

winding house, page 97; Morleys' hosiery factory, page 98; Playworld, page 105; Tumble Town, page 106.

Ollerton
Rufford Country Park, page 49; Rufford Abbey, page 61; Ollerton watermill, page 101.

In the locality: Sherwood Forest Country Park, page 50; Kirton Wood, page 52; Clipstone Forest, page 53; Bothamsall Castle, page 56; Egmanton Castle, page 58; King John's Palace, page 58; Egmanton church, page 64; Laxton Visitor Centre, page 85; Sherwood Forest Amusement Park, page 105; Sherwood Forest Farm Park, page 105; World of Robin Hood, page 106.

Ossington
Church of the Holy Rood, page 68.

Oxton
Not only is Oldox Camp evidence of early settlement in the area, but an Anglo-Saxon barrow was also excavated nearby. In medieval times it was uncertain whether Oxton lay just inside or just outside the boundary of Sherwood Forest. The church, St Peter and St Paul, has a Norman chancel and a rare pillar piscina of the same date. The nave is early fourteenth-century and the tower, which is partly built into it, only slightly later. The battlements and clerestory are fifteenth-century. The south aisle was rebuilt in the eighteenth century and the north in 1898. Inside there is an effigy of a lawyer, fourteenth-century, and three fonts, one Norman, one fifteenth-century and one Restoration. The woodwork in the chancel — altar rails, choirstalls and screen — is seventeenth-century, with eighteenth-century box pews in the nave. The royal arms are those of George II, to which another I was added when George III became king. The hatchments bear the Sherbrooke arms, the family having been lords of the manor since the sixteenth century. Oxton still retains the feel of an estate village, even though the Hall was demolished in 1957.

Oldox Camp, page 60.
In the locality: Burntstump Country Park,

page 47; Blidworth Bottoms, page 53; Haywood Oaks, page 54; Painters' Paradise, page 83; Calverton framework knitters' cottages, page 97.

Papplewick

Church of St James, page 70; Papplewick Pumping Station, page 101.

Rampton

Sundown Kiddies Adventureland, page 105.

Ratcliffe on Soar

Church of the Holy Trinity, page 70.

Ravenshead

Thieves Wood and Harlow Wood, page 54; Longdale Craft Centre and Museum, page 92; Papplewick Pumping Station, page 101; Abbeydale Farm Centre, page 104.

Retford

Early closing, Wednesday; market days, Thursday and Saturday.

A market town since 1246, Retford is made up of East and West Retford, separated by the river Idle, and the village of Ordsall. In the eighteenth century there were attempts to increase the town's prosperity — unsuccessfully in a project to make the river navigable from Retford to Bawtry in 1719 and successfully in the diversion of the Great North Road, which then lay 2 miles (3 km) to the west, through the town by an Act of Parliament dated 1766. The modern A1 now runs about 4 miles (6.5 km) to the west. The construction of the Chesterfield Canal, which crosses the Idle by means of an aqueduct, brought yet more trade. The Market Square is the focal point of the town, with substantial Georgian houses on three sides. The Victorian Town Hall of 1868 on the south side expresses the pretensions of the citizens of the day rather than their taste. The Old Bank of 1887, next to it, is a little more sober in design. Churchgate leads off the Square and is dominated by the church, St Swithun. Of the medieval church only the north transept remains. The crossing tower collapsed in 1651 and much of the church had to be rebuilt. The

The church of St Swithun, Retford.

The Governor's House, Newark (see page 24).

northern side was largely rebuilt in 1855, and north and south porches were added. The stained glass is by many of the best Victorian makers: Hardman, Wailes, O'Connor, Kempe and Clayton & Bell. Opposite the church in Churchgate is Sloswicke's Hospital, an almshouse founded in 1657, rebuilt in the early nineteenth century with a classical pediment and Gothick windows. Across the ring road, Arlington Way, is a Gothick cottage of 1834, with elaborate detail including statues on brackets with canopies above them either side of the first-floor windows. To the south of the church, in Chapelgate is Ye Olde Sun dating back to the sixteenth century. Nearby is a 24-pounder Russian cannon captured at Sebastopol in 1858. Grove Street also leads off the Market Square and here are two handsome Georgian houses that have not been altered by the addition of shop-fronts: Poplar House (number 25) and Amcott House, which now houses the Bassetlaw Museum. Here too

A relic of the Crimean War at Retford: a cannon captured at Sebastopol.

is the Methodist church of 1880, by the same architects as the Town Hall, Bellamy & Hardy of Lincoln, and similarly overambitious for a market town.

The medieval church of West Retford, St Michael, is notable for the unusually attractive way its spire is built on to the tower. All Saints, Ordsall, is thirteenth-century, though this is obscured by T. C. Hine's restoration of 1876. It retains its medieval screen.

Bassetlaw Museum, page 93.

In the locality: Clumber Park and church, pages 47 and 64; Daneshill Lakes, page 47; Clarborough Tunnel, page 51; Eaton Wood, page 52; Bothamsall Castle, page 56; Kingshaugh, page 58; Mattersey Priory, page 59; churches at Blyth, page 63; and East Markham, page 64; Littleborough Toll Cottage, page 98; North Leverton windmill, page 99; Wetlands Waterfowl Reserve, page 106; World of Robin Hood, page 106.

Ruddington

Framework Knitters' Museum, page 94; Village Museum, page 95.

Scarrington

The main attraction of this village is not a big house nor yet the church, although this bears the unusual dedication of St John of Beverley and has one of the dozen Restoration fonts in the county. It is a stack of about fifty thousand horseshoes, some 17 feet (5 metres) high, that the village blacksmith built of discarded shoes between 1945 and 1965. Together with the nearby pinfold, or pound for stray cattle, it makes a curious relic of the rural past.

In the locality: Cranmer's Mound, page 56; Thoroton dovecote, page 62.

Sibthorpe

Sibthorpe dovecote, page 62.

South Scarle

This is an attractive little village on the borders with Lincolnshire. The church, St Helen, appears mainly late medieval on the outside, but inside there are a fine Norman arcade like that at South Collingham and a thirteenth-century south arcade and chancel with a double piscina. The screen is fifteenth-

The Saracen's Head in Southwell, where King Charles I surrendered to the Scots.

century, as are some of the pews with poppy-heads. Moses and Aaron adorn the Ten Commandments. There is an incised slab to William Meryng (*c*.1510), another member of the local family some of whose other monuments may be seen at East Markham, Newark, South Collingham and Sutton on Trent. The most unusual item in the church is the vamping horn, similar to that at East Leake and one of only nine in England. There are several seventeenth-century houses in the village, including the Old Vicarage and Church Farmhouse. Among the outbuildings of Beeches Farm is a two-storey stone dovecote with a pyramidal roof of pantiles.

Southwell
Early closing, Wednesday; market day, Saturday.
Known throughout Nottinghamshire as 'Suthell', the town's name is perversely pronounced as it is written by the locals. It is a most attractive town with more than a touch of Barchester to it. It is dominated by the Minster, with which most of the buildings around are, or were, connected. To the east is

the Vicars' Court and the Residence. The latter was built *c*.1690 and the Vicars' Court on either side *c*.1780, blending in remarkably well. To the north, along Church Street, are six of the Prebends — houses of the Prebendaries, or canons, of the Minster. There were at one time sixteen in the town, all except one being named after the manors from which their revenues come. South Muskham Prebend is basically medieval with an early nineteenth-century façade. Normanton Prebend was rebuilt with a handsome Doric porch in about 1765 and Woodborough Prebend (now called Ashleigh) is another old house with a façade of about 1819. Oxton I (now Cranfield House) is a splendid Queen Anne building, 1709, of two storeys with a hipped roof and dormers, and with pediments over the front door and corresponding first-floor window. North Muskham is probably seventeenth-century, largely rebuilt in about 1769 with a more fashionable façade added forty years later. Norwell Overhall (divided into Minster Lodge and the National Westminster Bank) is another medieval house, of stone, with a brick façade of 1784.

Southwell Minster from the south (see page 70).

(Opposite) The west front of Southwell Minster.

In Westgate are three more: Sacrista Prebend, again a basically eighteenth-century house with a later Gothick façade; Rampton, early seventeenth-century updated with stucco and sash windows around 1800; and Dunham, another old house with a façade of about 1780 and a Regency extension of 1805. Near Sacrista Prebend are the Assembly Rooms of 1805, which have been taken over by the Saracen's Head. The old part of this coaching inn is sixteenth-century, timber-framed on the upper floor. Originally this projected over the ground floor, which was extended forward in 1693. It was known as the King's Arms when Charles I spent his last hours of freedom here in 1646. The name was changed shortly after his execution. There are seventeenth-century buildings in Queen Street and King Street but far more in the town are Georgian.

To the north of the town is the spacious Burgage Green. Burgage Manor is a fine Regency House where Byron and his mother lived from 1803 to 1807. The Burgage is another substantial Georgian property whereas the Grey House, of white brick, is Victorian. Elmfield House, near the war memorial, is early eighteenth-century. The heavy archway on the west side of the green belongs to the former House of Correction of 1807. It is odd that such a prosperous neighbourhood should have tolerated a prison on its doorstep. It became a lace factory in 1880.

To the south of the Minster are the mainly fourteenth- and fifteenth-century ruins of the palace of the Archbishops of York. That part immediately by the south door has been restored to church use and the whole of the western side now forms the present Bishop's Palace. Further south still, in Nottingham Road, is the Baptist chapel, a three-storey building with a semicircular bay in the centre. It was built in 1808 as the workhouse and sold to the Baptists in 1839 since a much bigger workhouse (now called Greet House) had been built in 1824 on the road to Upton.

Farnsfield to Southwell Trail, page 53; **Southwell Minster**, page 70; **Norwood Park**, page 81; **Bramley Apple Display**, page 104.

In the locality: Bleasby dovecote, page 56; Oldox Camp, page 60; Thurgarton Priory, page 74; British Horological Institute, page 95; *Fiskerton Mill, page 98; Reg Taylor's Swan Sanctuary, page 105.*

Spalford
Spalford Warren, page 53.

Stapleford
The Hemlockstone, page 52; church cross, page 62; framework knitters' cottages, page 102.

In the locality: Attenborough Gravel Pits, page 50; Chilwell Meadow, page 51; Anglo-Scotian Mills, page 96.

Staunton in the Vale
The Vale of Belvoir is the setting for a number of pretty villages, of which Staunton is one, close to the Three Shires Bush that marks the point at which Leicestershire, Lincolnshire and Nottinghamshire meet. The place is steeped in history: a Romano-British settlement was discovered here and the Staunton family, which still owns the Hall, is said to have lived here since 1041. The Hall is sixteenth-century, with late Georgian additions, and is reputed to be the inspiration for 'Willingham' in Sir Walter Scott's *Heart of Midlothian*. The church was restored in 1853 but the north aisle, with its fourteenth-century doorway and arcades, and the slightly later massive tower were hardly touched. The Norman font is the oldest feature but there are several early Staunton monuments, of which the best is to Sir William (died 1326), depicting his fully armed upper half and feet. Later members are commemorated by wall tablets, one of which, to Job Staunton Charlton and his wife, is by Westmacott. The chancel screen is remarkably well preserved and its inscription invites one to 'pray for the saule of Mayster Symon Yates', parson of the church, who erected it at his own expense in 1519. The barrel organ dates from 1832.

Strelley
Oldmoor Wood, page 52; church of All Saints, page 72.

Sutton Bonington
This must be an ancient settlement, since a pagan Anglo-Saxon cemetery was excavated

here. Now it is a long straggling village, but this is hardly surprising since it was originally two hamlets. The church of St Michael, Bonington, is mainly thirteenth- and fourteenth-century with a fifteenth-century spire and clerestory. The piers in the nave are surrounded by stone ledges for seating. The fourteenth-century font is unusual in that it has three rests for the candle, salt and baptismal service book. St Anne, Sutton, is a small thirteenth-century church, though somewhat restored. Inside is an alabaster knight of *c*.1475. Both churches have stained glass by Kempe.

There is a variety of interesting housing here. The oldest is a sixteenth-century timber-framed cottage with gables and projecting upper storey. Another, in Soar Lane, is dated 1661, the long windows on the first floor being a later alteration for the benefit of framework knitters. A late seventeenth-century stone house stands in Park Lane and there are some good brick houses in the Main Street. The Hall is eighteenth-century, built by Beaumont Parkyns, brother of Thomas Parkyns, the Wrestling Baronet of Bunny (page 15). Sutton Bonington had its own celebrity in William Riste (1743-73), the Nottinghamshire Giant, 7 feet 6½ inches (2.3 metres) tall, who was presented at court several times.

Sutton cum Lound
Wetlands Waterfowl Reserve and Exotic Bird Park, page 106.

Sutton in Ashfield
Early closing, Wednesday; market days, Friday and Saturday.
Once a small village, Sutton has grown much bigger as a result of industry and coal mining but has not gained any buildings of interest. There are a few seventeenth- and eighteenth-century houses in the older part of the town, near the church, otherwise it is only the church itself, St Mary Magdalene, that is worth a visit. It has Norman work in the west wall, and the pillar piscina is of a similar date. The arcades are thirteenth-century and one capital has a particularly delicate carving of heads. The spire is fourteenth-century, the clerestory

fifteenth-century and the whole church was restored in Victorian times.

In the locality: Thieves Wood and Harlow Wood, page 54; Teversal church, page 72; Kings Mill viaduct, page 98.

Sutton on Trent
One of the larger villages in this part of the Trent valley, Sutton benefits considerably from having been bypassed by the A1. Alongside the Trent are 300 acres (121 hectares) of grazing land, known as The Holmes, made up of 'cattle gaits' — grazing rights owned by a number of people that are rented out at the annual Gait Letting. At the south end of the village is a brick windmill of about 1814, lacking its sails and fantail. There are some pleasant inns and houses, including a timber-framed cottage, but it is All Saints church that is the main attraction. It is recorded in the Domesday Book and Saxon and early Norman work has been found at the base of the tower, which is mainly thirteenth-century with a slightly later top stage. The rest of the church is of about this date, except for the early sixteenth-century clerestory and the Meryng chapel on the south side of the chancel, built in about 1520. This is far more ornate with elaborate battlements, pinnacles and gargoyles. Inside are seven similar brackets for statues of saints and a Purbeck marble altar tomb, assumed to be that of Sir William Meryng, who died in 1537. The rood screen and loft between the chapel and the south aisle are carved with fine tracery and friezes of leaves, with the Meryng arms. In the chancel are fifteenth-century bench ends with poppyheads of birds and a variety of faces.

In the locality: Ossington church, page 68.

Teversal
Church of St Catherine, page 72.

Thoroton
Thoroton dovecote, page 62.

Thurgarton
Thurgarton Priory, page 74.

Torworth
Daneshill Lakes, page 47.

Nottingham Castle (see page 81).

(Opposite) The statue of Robin Hood by James Woodford stands below Nottingham Castle.

Tuxford

Daniel Defoe found this a 'dirty little market town', but he may have visited it before a major fire in 1702 destroyed many of the old buildings. The church, St Nicholas, survived. The nave, aisles and lower part of the tower are thirteenth-century and the upper stages and spire fourteenth-century. The south porch was added in the following century, as was the clerestory of about 1475, with battlements and a turret at the south-east corner for the stairs leading to the rood loft. The chancel was rebuilt by the prior of Newstead Abbey in 1495 and has a fine east window and a variety of gargoyles. The upper part of the rood screen is also fifteenth-century, the rest being modern, but the most striking, if not the most beautiful, woodwork in the church is the canopy over the font, made by Francis Turner in 1673. The more modest font cover is of the same date, and the font is one of the dozen in the county that were put up within a couple of

The church of St Nicholas, Tuxford.

years of the Restoration in 1660. The chapel in the south aisle was presumably dedicated to St Lawrence since there is here a rather mutilated statue of him with the grid on which he was roasted, and he is also depicted in the fifteenth-century stained glass. There are two poorly preserved fourteenth-century monuments and one to Sir John White (died 1625) and his wife Dorothea, who lies slightly below him. A wall monument commemorates Captain C. L. White, who died fighting the French at Bayonne in 1814. There are also two hatchments to the White family.

Across the road from the church is the old grammar school, now a public library, founded in 1609 by Charles Read, who had inscribed above the door: 'What God hath built let no man destroy.' Two storeys high, built of brick with a hipped roof and pretentious doorway, it looks more like a merchant's house. In the Market Place stands the Newcastle Arms, a large Georgian hotel, recalling the town's importance as a coaching stop on the Great North Road, and an attractive combined street light and signpost of 1897 points the way. A brick lock-up in Newcastle Street, dated 1823, took care of the less desirable travellers. North of the town is Longbottoms Mill and to the south is another nineteenth-century windmill, Weston Mill, built of brick, four storeys high, but in less good condition.

Longbottoms Mill, page 98.

In the locality: Kirton Wood, page 52; Bothamsall Castle, page 56; Egmanton Castle, page 58; Kingshaugh, page 58; churches at East Markham, page 64; Egmanton, page 64; Fledborough, page 64; and Ossington, page 68; World of Robin Hood, page 106.

Upton

British Horological Institute, page 95.

Warsop
Market day, Friday.

This is now quite a large village, its expansion due to the local collieries. Church Warsop, north of the river Meden, represents the old settlement. The church, St Peter and St Paul, has a Norman tower, with a zigzag decoration on its interior arch. The rest of the

The maypole on the village green at Wellow.

church is largely thirteenth- and fourteenth-century, with the vestry, which was presumably once a chantry chapel, an early sixteenth-century addition. Nearby is the Old Hall, with medieval features, though jumbled up in the Victorian restoration. The seventeenth-century barn has been converted into a parish centre. On the river Meden is an eighteenth-century watermill, for grinding corn, and on the road to Edwinstowe there is a stone windmill, without cap or sails.

In the locality: Clipstone Forest, page 53; Meden Trail, page 54; Cuckney Castle, page 58; King John's Palace, page 58.

Welbeck
Creswell Crags, page 56.

Wellow
One of the prettiest villages in the county, Wellow is probably most famous for its green and permanent maypole. Earlier ones were of timber from Sherwood Forest, but the present one is steel, erected in 1976. The scene was not always so idyllic; to the north-east and south-east of the village are the remains of defensive earthworks, possibly made to protect both people and cattle during squabbles with Rufford Abbey. Further north-east are the earthworks of Jordan Castle, fortified by Richard Foliot and his son Jordan in 1264. It was he who obtained permission, in 1268, for a weekly market and annual fair at Wellow, which may be the origin of the maypole dancing here. The parish church, St Swithin, was thoroughly restored in 1878, but the bottom storey of the tower is twelfth-century and the font Norman. The east window, also of 1878, is by Kempe. None of the houses in the village is of outstanding architectural merit but the overall effect of the seventeenth- and eighteenth-century brick and pantile and the odd timber-framed cottages is most pleasing.

In the locality: Rufford Country Park, page 49; Rufford Abbey, page 61; Ollerton watermill, page 101.

West Stockwith
This is another village which has little to show of architectural interest other than the

church, but its setting, where the Chesterfield Canal and the river Idle meet the Trent, is irresistible. It was an inland port, even before the canal was opened to the Trent in 1777, though its subsequent decline was closely linked to that of the canal. As well as trading and warehousing, West Stockwith was a centre for boatbuilding. One of its inhabitants, William Huntingdon, who died in 1722, made sufficient money as a 'ship carpenter' to found several charities and build the village church. It is small and neat, of red brick, a perfect example of its period, with his monument in a prominent position inside. He reclines on his left elbow, displaying in his right hand the plan of a sailing ship. Another relic of that era is Ropery House, dated 1741, once part of a rope-walk. The boats now to be seen in the canal basin and on the Trent are more for pleasure than for business.

Miniature World Museum, page 95.

In the locality: Trent Valley Way, page 55.

Whatton
Church of St John of Beverley, page 74.

Wilford
Wilford Bridge tollhouse, page 103.

Willoughby on the Wolds
Church of St Mary and All Saints, page 74.

Winkburn
The Wink is the name of the stream that flows just to the north of this tiny village, which consists of little more than church and hall. The latter was built of brick with stone quoins in the late seventeenth century, with an upper storey added a century later. Unpretentious, with good eighteenth-century interiors, it is open to the public by appointment (telephone: 0636 86465). The manor was formerly owned by the Knights Hospitallers, hence the dedication of the church to St John of Jerusalem. There is plenty of Norman work in the church, notably the tower arch with zigzag decoration and the doorway with beakhead ornament. The tower, too, is Norman, rebuilt in 1632, which is presumably when the pinnacles and battlements are added. It was also in the seventeenth century that the church was given

most of its fittings: the small font, the three-decker pulpit and the screen with the arch above blocked up. The altar rails and box pews are slightly later and the royal arms of George III are dated 1764. There is an incised slab to William Burnell, died 1570, and a wall monument with a kneeling effigy of another William Burnell, died 1609. Darcy Burnell died in 1774 and his monument consists of an urn on a pedestal flanked by Fame, with a portrait of the deceased, and an angel holding a torch upside down, signifying the life snuffed out.

Wollaton
Harrison's Plantation and Martin's Pond, page 52; church of St Leonard, page 75; Wollaton Hall, page 84; Natural History Museum, page 90; Nottingham Industrial Museum, page 91.

Woodborough
Fox Wood hillfort, page 58.

Worksop
Early closing, Thursday; market days, Wednesday, Friday and Saturday.

The town is noted for its Priory and Gatehouse but there is more to it than that. In the Market Place stands the Town Hall, built in 1851 as the Corn Exchange, and described then as 'a neat and useful building in the Italian style'. On the west side of the Market Place stands the timber-framed Old Ship, built in the late fifteenth or early sixteenth century but restored many times since then. Nearby is the former Lion Hotel, Georgian with Victorian wrought ironwork. To the south runs Park Street, which has a fine Georgian terrace, some eighteenth-century cottages and the Roman Catholic church of St Mary, built in 1838-9. To the east of the Market Place is Pottergate, which leads to the Priory. Devotees of Edwardian pub architecture will enjoy the terracotta and Burmantofts faience of the French Horn; others may prefer the Georgian style of Dunstan House, built by Henry Dunstan, Sheriff of Nottinghamshire in 1745. To the north lies Bridge Street, the pedestrianised shopping area, with, amongst other commercial buildings, two banks in neo-

Rufford Country Park, the lake and the mill (see page 49).

Sherwood Forest (see page 50).

classical style: the Trustee Savings of 1843 in stone, and the Yorkshire of 1859 in brick and stone. West of Bridge Street, running parallel to it, is Norfolk Street, with a terrace of millworkers' cottages built in stone, with some brick, in 1795. Between the two streets is Castle Hill, the site of Worksop's castle. Presumably it was originally built of timber and subsequently of stone, but by the time of Henry VIII nothing was left.

Two buildings away from the town centre are also of interest. Manor Lodge, north of the A60 to the west of the town, is a five-storey Elizabethan stone mansion that was originally even higher. The central section has two huge rooms, the Great Hall and the Great Chamber, both two storeys high. It was probably built by Robert Smythson, who also built Worksop Manor, for which it was a lodge, though it is not clear why such a large building should be necessary. More mundane is 7 Blyth Grove, a property owned by the National Trust and open by appointment (telephone: 0909 482380). Nothing has changed in this red brick semi-detached Edwardian house since the 1930s.

In Elizabethan times Worksop was noted for its liquorice and later for its malting industry. The Chesterfield Canal was opened in 1772 and the railway came in 1849. By 1898, when coal mining started at Manton Pit, Worksop had become more of an industrial centre than a country market town.

Hannah Park Wood, page 52; **Priory Gatehouse**, page 60; **Priory Church**, page 75; **Worksop Museum**, page 95; **Pickford's Depository**, page 102.

In the locality: Clumber Park and church, pages 47 and 64; Langold Country Park, page 49; Bothamsall Castle, page 56; Creswell Crags, page 56; Cuckney Castle, page 58; churches at Blyth, page 63; and Carlton in Lindrick, page 63; Hodsock Priory Gardens, page 78; Carlton Mill, page 98.

The lime trees lining the Duke's Drive in Clumber Park.

3
The countryside

Country parks

Nottinghamshire is well supplied with country parks, which act not only as nature reserves but provide outdoor leisure facilities as well.

Bestwood Country Park, Bestwood, Nottingham (OS 129: SK 572463). Nottinghamshire County Council and Gedling Borough Council.

Part of this site is the remnant of one of the royal deer parks, the rest being a reclaimed spoil tip from Bestwood colliery. Since the top of the old tip has been colonised by nature, rather than with any human assistance, this is of particular interest to biologists. It is 450 acres (182 hectares) in all and such a varied landscape supports a surprising range of birds and butterflies. Walkers, cyclists and horse-riders are all welcome in the park, a way-faring course has been set up and there is scope for other outdoor activities.

Burntstump Country Park, Arnold (OS 120: SK 576505). Gedling Borough Council.

This park is about 65 acres (26.5 hectares), with open space for picnics and games and woodland of beech, birch and oak with some rhododendrons that are very attractive in late spring.

Clumber Park, Worksop S80 3AZ (OS 120: SK 625745). Telephone: 0909 476653. National Trust.

Open daily; Vineries open summer weekends only. Café and restaurant.

The story of Clumber Park began in 1707 when permission was given to the third Duke of Newcastle to enclose part of Sherwood Forest as a hunting park for Queen Anne. In the 1760s the first house was built with lodges and gates at the entrances to the park and a lake was created from the river Poulter, crossed by a fine classical bridge. The house was altered and extended early in the nine-teenth century but much of it was burnt down in 1879. It was rebuilt in an Italianate style but demolished only sixty years later when upkeep became impossible. Of the house only the Duke's Study survives at the southern tip of the estate offices. The eighteenth-century red-brick coach-house has an imposing pediment and cupola and the stable block includes other outbuildings such as the brewhouse. Not far away are the Vineries, Fig House and Palm House, a range of late nineteenth-century glasshouses with an exhibition of garden tools. They form one side of the walled kitchen garden. To the east of the stables is the chapel (page 64), and to the south is the ground plan of the house.

Along the lake are the pleasure grounds with rhododendrons and specimen trees, and a small Roman temple with its Greek counterpart across the lake. The park covers over 3800 acres (1918 hectares), with many coniferous plantations around the boundary but plenty of deciduous trees in the old parkland.

Some of the park is farmed, but the grassland attracts about twenty species of butterfly and the heathland is good habitat for reptiles. Perhaps the most impressive feature of the park, however, is the 3 mile (5 km) Duke's Drive lined on either side with a double row of lime trees.

Colwick Country Park, Colwick (OS 129: SK 608399). Nottingham City Council.

There are 250 acres (101 hectares) of parkland here, of which over 90 acres (36.5 hectares) is under water. As at Attenborough and Holme Pierrepont, these are former gravel workings. A nature reserve has been established here and there are facilities for fishing, sailing, rowing, sailboards and swimming.

Daneshill Lakes, Torworth (OS 120: SK 668866). Nottinghamshire County Council and Nottinghamshire Wildlife Trust. Warden on site (telephone: 0777 818196).

Disused gravel workings together with land formerly belonging to the Royal Ordnance Factory have been made into a combined nature reserve and leisure facility. On the south side of the road between Torworth and Lound is a site of about 80 acres (32 hectares), mainly lakes used for fishing, sailing, canoeing and windsurfing, with one part maintained as a schools nature reserve.

To the north side of the road a smaller area, about 40 acres (16 hectares) is kept solely as a nature reserve. This is more wooded but has some scrub and wet grassland as well as lakes. Among the flowering plants are several orchids, and a number of butterflies, such as meadow brown, ringlet, gatekeeper, common blue and brimstone, may be seen here. It is particularly noted for its bird life including kingfishers, all three species of woodpecker, sedge and willow warblers, whitethroat, blackcap and a variety of wildfowl and waders.

Holme Pierrepont Country Park and National Water Sports Centre, Adbolton Lane, Holme Pierrepont, Nottingham NG12 2LU (OS 129: SK 608387). Telephone: 0602 821212. Nottinghamshire County Council. *Open daily from dawn to dusk, except Christmas Day.*

Holme Pierrepont is best known for the National Water Sports Centre, with 90 out of 270 acres (36.5 out of 109 hectares) being water. There is a $1^1/4$ mile (2 km) rowing and canoeing course, which is also used for dinghy and board sailing, power-boat racing and water-skiing. The famous white-water slalom course is a challenge for canoeists. There is fishing along the bank of the Trent and in the 2000 metres regatta course. There are two nature reserves, one specially for the benefit of the wheelchair-bound, with hides for watching the many species of birds here, wildfowl in particular.

Langold Country Park and Dyscarr Wood, Langold (OS 120: SK 581865 and 581868). Telephone: 0909 475531. Bassetlaw District Council and Nottinghamshire Wildlife Trust.

The lake in this 74 acre (30 hectare) country park was made early in the nineteenth century to be the centrepiece in the grounds of a country house that was never built. Some of the land is mature parkland and some was reclaimed from the shale tips and railway sidings of the old Costhorpe mine. This provides a wide variety of flora and fauna, including meadow flowers and marsh marigolds and birds from water rails to woodpeckers. There is ancient woodland too, since Dyscarr Wood straddles the track from Langold to Letwell (South Yorkshire), and the southern part adjoins the country park. It is one of the best examples of an ash and wych-elm wood in the county. Plants include ramsons, wood melick, twayblade and orchids, and about fifty species of bird have been recorded here. Among the fourteen species of butterfly are small copper and orange tip. An interesting feature is the boundary ditch and bank system that runs through the wood separating Nottinghamshire and the former West Riding of Yorkshire.

Rufford Country Park, Ollerton (OS 120: SK 643648). Nottinghamshire County Council. Telephone: 0623 824153.

The grounds of Rufford Abbey (page 61), 172 acres (69.6 hectares) in all, are partly cultivated and partly wild. By the house are nine formal gardens, of which the herb garden is perhaps the most interesting. These are also the setting for the permanent sculpture collection. Nearby are an arboretum and a field set aside for a flock of Mouflon sheep. The Lime Avenue is majestic with its mature trees, and the lake, created in the eighteenth century, is home to a variety of wildfowl, including Canada geese. At the southern end of Broad Ride are the graves of animals belonging to former owners of Rufford. The racehorse Cremorne, winner of the Derby in 1872, is buried here. Other curiosities in the grounds are two icehouses built around 1820 to preserve a supply of ice beyond the winter months. In the wilder parts are hides for

(Opposite) The canoe slalom course at Holme Pierrepont.

birdwatchers and a portion of the lake has been designated a bird sanctuary. At the northern end of the lake is the late eighteenth-century corn mill with a saw mill added in a similar style in 1860. This houses an exhibition centre where a different display illustrating Nottinghamshire history is mounted every year. Car parking is free except at summer weekends and Bank Holidays.

Sherwood Forest Country Park and Visitor Centre, Edwinstowe, Mansfield NG21 9HN (OS 120: SK 627677). Nottinghamshire County Council. Telephone: 0623 823202.

Sherwood Forest originally covered about 100,000 acres (40,470 hectares). The Country Park accounts for 450 acres (182 hectares). The Visitor Centre sets the scene with an exhibition about Robin Hood and Sherwood Forest; thereafter the forest speaks for itself. The ancient gnarled 'stag-headed' oaks are very evocative. The Major Oak is the most famous, 65 feet (19.8 metres) in height and 33 feet (10.0 metres) in circumference. It is between six hundred and seven hundred years old. The silver birches have been here just as long. It is not surprising that in such a place over two hundred types of fungus, 218

species of spider and over a thousand varieties of beetle can be found. As well as more common birds, woodpeckers, tree creepers and jays may be seen. Fallow deer are fairly common but red and roe deer, although present, are rarely visible. A number of suggested routes around the forest have been marked out and a wayfaring course is available for those who prefer to find their own way. From April to October there is a fairground. There are also facilities for the disabled, a ranger information post and cricket pitch. Car parking is free except at summer weekends and Bank Holidays.

Nature reserves

The Nottinghamshire Wildlife Trust has been very active and manages nearly fifty nature reserves, of which over a third are open to the public. The Woodlands Trust has five, three of which are open.

Attenborough Gravel Pits, Attenborough (OS 129: SK 521343). Nottinghamshire Wildlife Trust.

These disused gravel pits were one of the first nature reserves run by the Trust and were opened in 1966, appropriately by Sir David Attenborough. The 360 acres (145.5 hectares)

'Ewe and Man on Bench', a sculpture by Siobhan Coppinger in Rufford Country Park.

The Major Oak in Sherwood Forest.

are mainly lake but with some scrub and grassland. There is a wide variety of fish, insects and amphibians, but the reserve is particularly noted for its bird life. Wildfowl include sawbills, sea-ducks, garganey and cormorants and all the British grebes have been recorded here. It is also suitable habitat for several species of warbler. Even on a casual stroll along the nature trail, a heron or kingfisher may be seen.

Brecks Plantation and Glapton Wood, Clifton (OS 129: SK 553333 and 549339). Nottinghamshire Wildlife Trust.

Brecks Plantation, a 6 acre (2.5 hectare) site, was planted as mixed woodland at the end of the nineteenth century with a later addition of conifers. Glapton Wood is smaller, only 3½ acres (1.5 hectares), but older and mainly of oak, bordered by grassland. There is nothing of outstanding interest here but they are a valued amenity for the local population.

Bunny Old Wood West, Bunny (OS 129: SK 585285). Nottinghamshire Wildlife Trust.

Entry is by the public footpath that runs south from Bunny through the wood towards Wysall.

Bunny Wood is 38½ acres (26.5 hectares) of ancient woodland, mentioned in the Domesday Book, and mainly consisting now of elm, oak, ash and field maple. Thirty species of bird have been recorded and ten of butterfly, including the white letter hairstreak.

Chilwell Meadow, Chilwell (OS 129: SK 520357). Nottinghamshire Wildlife Trust.

Although only 2½ acres (1 hectare), this is one of the few wet meadows left in the Trent valley, with a wide variety of plants, including the common spotted orchid and marsh arrow grass.

Clarborough Tunnel, Clarborough (OS 120: SK 756826). Nottinghamshire Wildlife Trust.

This reserve covering 13 acres (5 hectares) runs alongside a railway cutting and above a tunnel on the Retford to Gainsborough line. The track was built for the Manchester, Sheffield and Lincolnshire Railway Company in 1849 and the site has been undisturbed since then. There are areas of dense woodland, scrub and grassland. The last, being rich in lime, is good for a number of plants, notably several species of orchid. These in turn attract colourful butterflies. There is also a small pond, frequented by great crested newts.

Eaton Wood, Eaton (OS 120: SK 727772). Nottinghamshire Wildlife Trust.

The area was recorded in the Domesday Book as pasture woodland and there is still some ridge and furrow to be seen, while the ditch and bank on the eastern edge forms the parish boundary between Eaton and Headon. The wood is mainly ash, elm and hazel with a sprinkling of oak and silver birch, and more recent pine and beech. It is more important for its plant life — moschatel, yellow archangel, herb paris and several orchids, as well as the more common primroses and bluebells.

Fairham Brook, Clifton (OS 129: SK 562338). Nottinghamshire Wildlife Trust.

This reserve comprises 26 acres (10.5 hectares) of lowland fen bog and meadow alongside the brook.

Hannah Park Wood, Worksop (OS 120: SK 590773). Woodland Trust.

The 14 acre (5.5 hectare) wood is a remnant of the northern edge of Sherwood Forest and is mainly oak and beech, with a small area of yew.

Harrison's Plantation and Martin's Pond, Wollaton (OS 129: SK 530403 and 527401). Nottinghamshire Wildlife Trust.

Martin's Pond, a site of 11 acres (4.5 hectares), is thought to be the first Local Nature Reserve declared in a city, after it was saved from a proposal to turn it into a car park. It is certainly old and may have been a medieval fishpond for Wollaton Hall. Over 150 flowering plants have been recorded and over seventy species of bird, including water rail and spotted crake — a remarkable achievement for a reserve within the city. Harrison's Plantation, 6 acres (2.5 hectares), is next to Martin's Pond and is mixed woodland going back at least to the mid eighteenth century. It is mainly sycamore, ash, wild cherry and oak. At the east end is Raleigh Pond, a former

claypit where mallard and Canada geese breed.

The Hemlockstone, Stapleford (OS 129: SK 499388).

This notable landmark has no sinister connections with poison. Its name simply means 'the stone in the border enclosure'. Despite this, local legends associate it with the Druids or even the devil, who is supposed to have thrown it at Lenton Priory, but missed! It is a red sandstone outcrop, 31 feet (9.5 metres) high, with a harder pebbly stone cap which has preserved it from weathering.

Kirton Wood, Kirton (OS 120: SK 708687). Nottinghamshire Wildlife Trust.

The trees in this 46 acre (18.5 hectare) wood were planted only in the late 1930s, but it is much older in origin. It is mainly ash and wych elm with hazel, dogwood and field maple. The flora includes several species of orchid and the bird life is varied, with sparrowhawks, spotted flycatchers and woodcock. A nature trail has been devised around the wood.

Oldmoor Wood, Strelley (OS 129: SK 499421). Woodland Trust.

This mainly broad-leaved wood covers 38 acres (15.5 hectares) with oak, ash, beech and sycamore and was planted in the 1790s to provide timber and cover for game. Birds to be found here include woodpeckers, jays and redpolls. It is also good habitat for moths and butterflies, such as the speckled wood. Among the plants are common hemp-nettle and hedge woundwort. There are also several ponds here. It has two smaller satellites — Holly Copse (501424) and Brickyard Plantation (493419), which has no public access.

Quarry Holes Plantation, Cinderhill, Nottingham (OS 129: SK 537433). Nottinghamshire Wildlife Trust.

This 5 acre (2 hectare) site gets its name from the Magnesian limestone quarry that was in use from the fifteenth century to the nineteenth. It is mainly mixed woodland with sycamore and ash, and some areas of scrub and grassland.

Seller's Wood, Bulwell (OS 129: SK 524454). Nottinghamshire Wildlife Trust.

Just outside the city boundary, this 35 acre (14 hectare) wood has soil ranging from acid to lime-rich with flora to match. Some of it is ancient woodland, and some, having been cleared in the past, has reverted. Ash, elm and sycamore are in abundance, with some birch, oak, poplar and willow. Flowers include giant bellflower and early purple orchid. Ponds and disused claypits contain a variety of aquatic animals and plants. The scrub is particularly good for butterflies and moths. A nature trail has been devised to show its best features.

Spalford Warren, Spalford (OS 121: SK 827678). Nottinghamshire Wildlife Trust.

In medieval times this area was used for rearing rabbits, hence its name. It is heathland, unusual for the county, and, although the Forestry Commission made an unsuccessful attempt to plant the 90 acre (36.5 hectare) site with conifers, much of the heath still remains.

The Hemlockstone.

Heather, gorse and broom abound but rarer plants like field mouse-ear and shepherd's cress may be found. Lizards are at home here and there are a number of butterflies to be seen.

Spa Ponds, New Clipstone (OS 120: SK 572628). Nottinghamshire Wildlife Trust.

Packman's Way, a bridlepath leading north from Newlands, runs right through this 16 acre (6.5 hectare) reserve. It consists of four ponds, three medieval and one modern, which are noted for dragonflies, though interesting birds such as kingfisher and little grebe may also be seen.

Walks and forest trails

Walkers are well provided for, with walks ranging from forest trails of only a mile (1.6 km) to long-distance footpaths. The County Council and some borough and district councils produce leaflets of suggested walks and several books are available. In addition the old canal system offers interesting rambling, particularly the disused Nottingham to Grantham canal.

Blidworth Bottoms, Blidworth (OS 120: SK 596543), Forestry Commission.

This is mixed woodland with two waymarked walks and picnic areas.

Clipstone Forest, Clipstone (OS 120: SK 614645). Forestry Commission.

Only a stone's throw from King John's Palace (page 58), this would have been good hunting country for the royal parties that stayed there. It is still the best place in Sherwood Forest to see fallow deer. Now there are plantations of conifers and deciduous trees with two waymarked walks, a 6 mile (10 km) cycle route and picnic places.

The Farnsfield to Southwell Trail. Car parks in Southwell, along the road to Normanton, and at Farnsfield and Kirklington stations. Nottinghamshire County Council.

The Midland Railway planned a line from Southwell to Mansfield as early as 1842, but it did not open until 1871 and was only single-track. Not surprisingly it fell under the

Beeching axe in the 1960s and was designated a public footpath. As well as being a pleasant 4^1/2 mile (7 km) walk, it is of interest for its industrial archaeology: the station buildings and warehouse; the Farnsfield Waterworks of 1910; Maythorn Mills, a former cotton mill built in 1786; and Greet Lily Mill, a corn mill rebuilt after a fire in 1867, both on the river Greet. The plant life is varied since the ground ranges from acid to lime-rich soil and from wet to dry, and the mixture of scrub and mature trees provides good habitat for woodland birds.

Haywood Oaks, Blidworth (OS 120: SK 606549). Forestry Commission.

The two waymarked walks pass some of the largest oak trees in Sherwood, the Haywood Oaks, though the rest of the wood is mainly conifers.

The Little John Challenge Walk

This 28 mile (45 km) walk has been devised by John Merrill, who reckons it can be done in a day, allowing nine to twelve hours. Alternatively, it has been split into seven sections of around 4 miles (6.5 km) each for those who prefer gentler exercise. It is a circular walk around Sherwood Forest starting at Edwinstowe (page 18) and passing through Church Warsop (page 42) and Cuckney (page 58) to Creswell Crags (page 56). It continues via Welbeck and Clumber Park (page 47), Hardwick, Bothamsall (page 56), Robin Hood's Cave and Ollerton, before completing the circuit at Edwinstowe.

The Meden Trail, Mansfield Woodhouse (OS 120: SK 527647). Mansfield District Council and Nottinghamshire Wildlife Trust.

The Meden, Rowthorne and Teversal Trails, known collectively as the Pleasley Trails Network, all follow disused railway lines. Of the three only the Meden Trail of 1^1/2 miles (2.5 km) is managed by the Wildlife Trust. The limestone not only dictates the nature of the grassland, woodland and scrub but also makes for interesting caves and fissures. Among the plants here are wild basil, greater burnet saxifrage, guelder-rose and sanicle. Birds include nuthatch, hawfinch and

all three species of woodpecker. For those interested in industrial archaeology, not only is the old trackway important but alongside the trail are the now deserted mid nineteenth-century Viyella Mills, built on the site of an early cotton mill founded in 1785.

The Robin Hood Way

The Nottingham Wayfarers' Rambling Club celebrated its golden jubilee in 1982 and devised this 88 mile (142 km) walk to commemorate the event. It starts at Nottingham Castle (page 81), where the legendary hero is said to have been imprisoned, and, taking in a variety of other sites connected with him, as well as a number of country parks, meanders its way northwards to Edwinstowe church, where he is said to have married Maid Marian. For those who find the prospect of the complete walk too daunting, it is split into eighteen sections of between 3 and 6 miles (5 to 10 km). From the castle it runs to Wollaton Hall (page 84), past the Hemlockstone (page 52) and Strelley church (page 72) to Kimberley. It continues to Blidworth (page 14) via Bestwood and Burntstump Country Parks (page 47) and Papplewick Pumping Station (page 101). A circular tour from Blidworth passes by Newstead Abbey (page 78) before going east and picking up the Farnsfield to Southwell Trail (page 53) as far as Kirklington. Thence it heads north, via Eakring, skirting Rufford Country Park (page 49), and almost touches Edwinstowe. The remainder of the walk is a lengthy circular route, anticlockwise, taking in part of Welbeck Park, Creswell Crags (page 56), Clumber Park (page 47) and the ruined chapel of the now demolished Haughton Hall, and returning through Sherwood Forest, passing both the Centre Tree and the Major Oak, until it finishes at the church of St Mary, Edwinstowe (page 18).

Thieves Wood and Harlow Wood, Ravenshead (OS 120: SK 541559 and 550568). Forestry Commission.

Thieves Wood offers two trails with eight information points and two picnic areas. In Harlow Wood, on the other side of the A60, the Friar Tuck Trail passes Fountaindale,

The Trent at Fiskerton Wharf.

associated with Friar Tuck's first meeting with Robin Hood, and Bessie Shepherd's Stone, which commemorates the victim of a particularly brutal murder in 1817.

The Trent Valley Way

This 84 mile (135 km) walk was opened in 1989 to celebrate the centenary of the County Council and is split into thirteen sections of between 3¹/2 and 10 miles (6.5 to 16 km), running either from Long Eaton or Thrumpton in the south and never straying more than a few miles from the river until it reaches West Stockwith (page 43) in the north. Having arrived at Nottingham, it continues via Holme Pierrepont Hall (page 78), Fiskerton Mill (page 98) and Kelham (page 21) to Newark (page 23). From there it goes to Holme by Newark (page 66), Collingham (page 17), Littleborough (page 22), North Leverton (page 99) and Gringley on the Hill (page 20), having passed four major power stations before finishing at the county boundary.

4

Ancient monuments

Barnby in the Willows dovecote, Dovecote Farm, Barnby in the Willows (OS 121: SK 859523).

There are three circular medieval dovecotes in the county, of which this is the smallest — only 15 feet (5 metres) high and 63 feet (19 metres) in circumference. The others are at Sibthorpe (page 62) and Thoroton (page 62). This is built of stone, with a tiled roof, and its nesting holes are also of stone, with some later ones made of brick and pantiles.

Barton in Fabis dovecote, Manor Farm, Barton in Fabis, Nottingham (OS 129: SK 523327).

This brick dovecote is all that remains of the family home of the Sacheverells and Sitwells. It was built in 1677 by William Sacheverell, who had his coat of arms carved inside. Half of its 1200 nesting boxes survive and it is the only octagonal dovecote in the county.

Bleasby dovecote, Manor Farm, Bleasby, Southwell (OS 129: SK 708498).

This eighteenth-century square dovecote is built of brick with a tiled roof. It has a central turret and two dormers as 'glovers', for the birds to fly in and out, and halfway up is a projecting brick ledge to prevent rats scaling the wall and getting in through the flight holes.

Bothamsall Castle, Bothamsall (OS 120: SK 671732).

This motte and bailey, overlooking the rivers Meden and Maun, is all that remains of the castle that was presumably built to guard the crossing points. There are no records of exactly when it was put up, but it was probably in the twelfth century.

Cranmer's Mound, Aslockton (OS 129: SK 743402).

A little east of the church and clearly visible from the public footpath that leads to Orston is the 16 feet (5 metres) high Norman motte known as Cranmer's Mound. Further east are two rectangular platforms with ditches around them, which seem to be the site of a later manor house where Archbishop Cranmer was born.

Creswell Crags, Crags Road, Welbeck, Worksop S80 3LH (OS 120: SK 536744). Telephone: 0909 720378.

Open daily March to October, Sundays only November to February.

The gorge forms the county boundary between Derbyshire and Nottinghamshire, and the Visitor Centre is run by Creswell Heritage Trust.

In the eighteenth century the primary importance of Creswell Crags was as picturesque scenery, used as a backdrop by George Stubbs (1724-1806) for some of his horse paintings. In 1872, however, prehistoric bones were found in Church Hole cave and attracted the attention of the Reverend Magens Mello, who went on to excavate further caves. His work, together with that of later archaeologists, gives a clear picture of the pattern of human occupation of the caves.

Around 43,000 BC they were the haunt of Neanderthal man, whose stone axes have been found along with the bones of hyenas, woolly rhinoceros and cave lions. As the ice age returned, the caves were deserted and not inhabited again until about 25,000 BC, when *Homo sapiens* moved in, as evidenced by his flint tools. The caves were again unoccupied for a long period until Upper Palaeolithic times. Between 8500 and 7000 BC they were home to a group of people with a culture sufficiently distinctive for them to be known today as 'Creswellian'. Not only have their tools been found, including a bone needle, but also a fine example of their art, a horse's head engraved on a fragment of rib bone.

The caves are unfortunately not open to the

Bothamsall Castle.

Creswell Crags.

public for safety reasons but can be seen as one walks around the lake that fills the bottom of the gorge. The Visitor Centre houses some of the finds from the site and puts them into context with an audio-visual display. The site is also of interest from a naturalist's point of view, with varied bird life and plants such as monkey flower and comfrey.

Cuckney Castle, Cuckney (OS 120: SK 566714).

In the troubled times of King Stephen (1135-54) many unauthorised fortifications were constructed and this mound, which forms what is now the western part of the churchyard, with a very marked ditch around it, was the site of a motte and bailey castle, built probably by Thomas de Cuckney. A mass burial of hundreds of skeletons discovered here in 1950 was once thought to have related to this period, although so large a battle is unlikely to have gone unrecorded. More recent research suggests that they were the bodies of those killed with King Edwin of Northumbria by the forces of Penda of Mercia at the battle of Heathfield (Hatfield) in 633.

Egmanton Castle, Egmanton (OS 120: SK 735690).

Egmanton was one of the 107 manors in Nottinghamshire held by Roger de Busli at the time of the Domesday Book and he may have been responsible for building this motte and bailey castle. The motte is very well preserved, 20 feet (6 metres) high and 460 feet (140 metres) in circumference, and the bank and ditch of the bailey can still be seen in places.

Fox Wood hillfort, Woodborough (OS 129: SK 613484).
The fort can be seen from a public footpath that runs inside the western end of the wood.

A number of hillforts were settled in the iron age along the Keuper marl hills on the southern edge of Sherwood Forest, among them Lodge Farm (Burton Joyce), Combs Farm (Farnsfield) and Fox Wood. The perimeter double bank and ditch are particularly well preserved on the north and west sides. The site has not been excavated but finds of

Roman pottery and evidence of a stone building suggest a continuous occupation.

Greasley Castle, Greasley (OS 129: SK 492471).

In 1340 Nicholas Cantilupe applied for permission from Edward III to fortify his manor house. Excavations carried out in 1901 suggested that the castle was square with towers at each corner. The plan of the moat can clearly be seen, particularly from the southeast corner of the adjacent churchyard, and from the road to Nuthall. The site is now occupied by an eighteenth-century farmhouse and some of the castle stonework has been incorporated into the outbuildings.

King John's Palace, Clipstone (OS 120: SK 604648).

Although King John seems to have spent some time at this hunting lodge, it was in existence before his reign and is recorded as early as 1164. It was quite a substantial complex, added to and rebuilt until the end of the fifteenth century. Thereafter it fell into disuse and was already in a state of disrepair by 1525. The walls now visible may be part of the undercroft for a new chamber and chapel that Edward I built in 1279. In 1290 he held a parliament at Clipstone, as indeed had King John in 1212. The palace seems a more likely venue for this than the decaying tree known as the Parliament Oak, about 2 miles (3 km) away.

Kingshaugh, Lincoln Road, Darlton, Newark NG22 0TP (OS 120: SK 764734). Telephone: 0777 871870.
May be seen by appointment.

The name means 'king's enclosure' in Anglo-Saxon, but its history goes back much further. Neolithic flints have been found here, along with an iron age quern and Romano-British pottery. The earthworks of banks and ditches extend to 7 acres (3 hectares) and probably go back to the iron age but much work was done in Norman times, when it was used as a hunting lodge. The first documentary evidence is in connection with John's rebellion in 1194. As king, John spent £550 4s 7d in 1211 on a new lodge and enclosure here, but this was abandoned as early as 1215. There is a seventeenth-century house on the site which incorporates medieval masonry up to 7 feet (2 metres) thick.

Lenton Priory, Nottingham (OS 120: SK 553387).

William Peverel founded this priory of Cluniac monks in the first decade of the twelfth century and it rapidly became the largest, wealthiest and most influential in the county, having the right of presentation to all three of Nottingham's parish churches. It had a colourful history, culminating in its seizure by attainder in 1538, when its prior, two monks and four lay brothers were executed for high treason. Only the base of a pillar and some foundations can be seen since the priory was almost totally destroyed and the site has been built over. What is now known as the Priory Church, although mainly Victorian, has a twelfth-century chancel which was probably the chapel of the priory hospital. The font from the old priory is now in Holy Trinity church, New Lenton. This is nearly square, carved in the middle of the twelfth century, and has scenes of the Baptism of Christ, the Crucifixion, the Entombment, the Resurrec-

tion and the three Marys at the tomb. It is one of the finest not only in Nottinghamshire, but also in England.

Mattersey Priory, Mattersey (OS 120: SK 703896). English Heritage.
Open daily .

Along a rough track to the east of the village stand the remains of a Gilbertine priory. This was the only house in the county belonging to the order founded by the long-lived St Gilbert of Sempringham (1083-1189). It was built on the banks of the river Idle in 1185 and endowed by Roger de Mattersey, though he cannot have been over-generous since it was never a wealthy establishment. Initially there were six canons and, though numbers did increase over the centuries, at its dissolution in 1538 only five lived there. The original monastery was destroyed by fire in 1279 and what is left of the dormitory range on the east side and the refectory on the south side date from the subsequent rebuilding. To the north side stand the walls of the fifteenth-century chapel which was dedicated to St Helen. In the parish church of Mattersey are two stone reliefs dating from about 1325 which probably came from the priory. They depict St

The ruins of Mattersey Priory.

Martin and the Beggar and the Finding of the True Cross by St Helen. The fine carving is in a similar style to the Easter sepulchres at Hawton (page 66) and Heckington, Lincolnshire.

Newark Castle, Castle Gate, Newark NG24 1BG. Telephone: 0636 611908.
Grounds open daily. Castle Story open all year (accessible to wheelchair users). Castle not open at present.

Historians agree that the castle was founded by Alexander, Bishop of Lincoln, around 1130. However, there is disagreement as to whether the two oldest parts of the castle, the gatehouse and the south tower, date from this time or if the first castle was a timber construction which was rebuilt in stone later in the twelfth century. Similarly there are different opinions as to where in the castle it was that King John died on 16th October 1216, with local tradition favouring the south tower and scholars the gatehouse. Certainly the latter is the most heavily fortified part of the castle. The wall alongside the river was rebuilt in the early fourteenth century with some alterations made late in the fifteenth century, notably the oriel window, and again late in the following century, as shown by the square-headed windows. Other features are the bottle dungeon in the north-west tower, the undercroft and the Water Gate.

Newark Castle was slighted in 1646, after the surrender of the Royalist garrison, in order to render it useless as a future defence. It is not, therefore, surprising that little is known of interior buildings or of much of the path of the curtain wall. A programme of archaeological investigations is being undertaken by Newark Castle Trust, who hope to find evidence of these parts of the castle. Although the castle is not open at present, the Castle Story, situated in the Gilstrap Centre, within the castle grounds, is a multi-media exhibition telling the story of Newark Castle.

Oldox Camp, Oxton (OS 120: SK 634532).

This is one of the largest iron age hillforts in the county, covering some 3 acres (1 hectare). It is surrounded by a single ditch and bank, except to the south-east corner, where it is double, protecting the main entrance.

Priory Gatehouse, Cheapside, Worksop (OS 120: SK 590788). Telephone: 0909 474173.

Although the priory was founded in 1103, the Gatehouse is early fourteenth-century, with two rooms either side of the central archway and the main hall above, in which visitors were offered hospitality, with a small room off it for the guest-master. The façade is striking, especially the large central window flanked by statues of saints, and the Trinity above. More lavish, however, is the slightly later porch to the shrine and Lady Chapel, which is still used. Only the angel of an Annunciation survives on the outside, but there is a modern statue of the Virgin and Child inside. Having spent most of the time since the Reformation as a schoolroom, it is now an arts centre and teashop.

Queen's Sconce, Newark (OS 120: SK 791531).

Newark was a strongly Royalist town in the Civil War, and particularly important for guarding the bridge over the Trent, since the only other bridge across the river in the county was at Nottingham, held by Parliament. The castle (see above) played a key part in the defence of the town but, to supplement it, two small forts were built: the King's Sconce, which has since disappeared, to the north-east, and the Queen's Sconce to the south-west. Queen Henrietta Maria brought reinforcements to the town after the first unsuccessful siege in 1643 so it was no empty compliment to name this fortification in her honour. It is a square earthwork with a bastion at each corner, and a hollow in the centre. It would serve both as an observation post and as a platform for cannon. There is a model of the Queen's Sconce in the Newark Museum in Appletongate (page 86).

The Parliamentarians also raised siege works, some of which survive to the west and north-west of the town, but the best preserved is by the river Devon to the south-west, at Hawton (SK 785513). This is a fortified camp, 375 by 270 feet (114 by 82 metres), built around the remains of a fifteenth-century moated manor site.

The monastic frater of Rufford Abbey and (right) the medieval dovecote at Sibthorpe.

Rufford Abbey, Ollerton (OS 120: SK 646647). Nottinghamshire County Council. Telephone: 0623 824153.
Open daily except Christmas Day and Boxing Day. Teashop.

Gilbert de Gant founded a Cistercian abbey here in 1146 as a daughter house of Rievaulx Abbey, but in 1536 it suffered the same fate as the other religious houses in England. It fell into the hands of the Earls of Shrewsbury and it was the sixth Earl, fourth husband of the redoubtable Bess of Hardwick, who turned it into a country house later in the sixteenth century. The property passed in 1626 to the Savile family, who lived here until 1938. Further improvements were carried out in 1679, when a north wing was built on the site of the abbey church. Some 160 years later the architect Salvin, who also designed Thoresby Hall, made more changes, notably in the Tudor-

style entrance to the west front, the cupola of the south wing and the coach-house, brewhouse and water tower. The Army took over the property in the Second World War and thereafter it became dilapidated, with the north and east wings being demolished in 1956.

The south wing still stands, with a noble stable block and orangery nearby, but it is the monastic remains that are most impressive. Entering by Salvin's west porch, the upper floor of the lay brothers' range is the dorter, or dormitory, from which night stairs descend to the ruins of the abbey church. At the south end of the lower floor is the frater, or refectory, with remains of the spoon and linen cupboards and a central arch in the south wall for a crucifix. The stone fireplace is a later addition. The small parlour, or recreation room, lies between the frater and the cellarium, or storehouse. The frater is groin-vaulted, with circular pillars, whereas the cellarium has a plain vaulted roof, with octagonal pillars. Both house displays on the history of Rufford. The grounds are now a country park (page 49).

Sibthorpe dovecote, Sibthorpe (OS 129: SK 765454).

This dovecote is, apart from the parish church, all that remains above ground of the college of priests founded here in the fourteenth century, though what may be its ground plan can be seen from the churchyard. Standing alone in the middle of a field, the dovecote appears even larger than it is — 30 feet (9 metres) in diameter and 60 feet (18 metres) high. It is circular, of stone, with a tiled roof and inside are 1260 nesting places arranged in 28 tiers.

Stapleford church cross, Stapleford (OS 129: SK 488374).

This 10 foot (3 metre) cross shaft is the best-preserved Saxon sculpture in the county. Opinion is divided as to its age, but the current view is that it may be as late as the eleventh century. It is largely decorated with interlaced patterns, but a winged figure may be seen on one side.

Thoroton dovecote, Ransomes Farm, Thoroton (OS 129: SK 763424).

Originally this medieval dovecote was higher, for it now consists only of the ground floor and half of the first floor. It is similar to that at Sibthorpe (see above), but smaller, built of stone, circular and with a thatched roof.

The church in Clumber Park.

5
Churches

Blyth: St Mary and St Martin.

The Benedictine priory at Blyth was founded in 1088 by Roger de Busli and work must have begun on the church shortly afterwards. Of this original Norman building the north aisle and nave remain, the latter shortened at each end but still magnificent in its lofty severity. Before the Dissolution it extended further to the east, with transepts, crossing and chancel, but this was all demolished since the townspeople had sufficient space for their requirements in the wide south aisle which was built to accommodate them and serve as the parish church at the end of the thirteenth century. The wall dividing the nave from the monastic part of the church was erected late in the fourteenth century and covered in its entirety by a wall painting of the Last Judgement. Much of this survives and it has been restored. Christ sits in majesty with his apostles as the dead rise from their coffins either to be greeted by angels on the left or carted off by demons to Hell in sacks or a wheelbarrow. The tower was started around 1400 but not completed until some hundred years later. Its battlements are attractively decorated with crocketed arches. The interior has some interesting fittings — an early seventeenth-century pulpit, late seventeenth-century font and a medieval poor-box. The best of the screens is in the south aisle, with paintings of saints, including Stephen, Edmund, Helena and Barbara. The earliest monument is that of a knight of the Fitzwilliam dynasty, *c*.1240, but more imposing is that portraying Edward Mellish (died 1703), reclining awkwardly. There are eight hatchments to various members of his family.

Carlton in Lindrick: St John the Evangelist.

At a distance the tower, architecturally the most important part of this church, appears fifteenth-century. It has buttresses, a belfry with Perpendicular windows, battlements and pinnacles. All of this is, however, an addition to the original late Saxon tower, with its characteristic features of twin bell-openings with rounded arches, and herringbone masonry below. What is now the west doorway, late Norman work, was originally the south door, moved in the nineteenth century when the south aisle was built. The north arcade and chancel windows are also Norman, as are the font and the tympanum of sun, moon and stars over the south chancel door. The fifteenth-century roof bosses display a variety of carving including the arms of Fitzhugh and Lord Dacre. Later local worthies were the Ramsdens — two of their hatchments hang here, along with the royal arms of George IV. There is an alabaster carving of the Trinity in the north aisle, of the kind for which Nottingham was famous in the middle ages, exporting them all over Europe. Below this is a stone altar thought to contain, beneath a lead seal in the centre, a relic of St Thomas à Becket.

Clifton: St Mary.

This is a large church, mainly of the fourteenth century, though the north arcade is of the late twelfth century and the north transept of the late fifteenth, altered when a chantry college was founded in 1476. The chancel was rebuilt in 1503. This is now separated from the rest of the church by a glazed screen, and the main altar was set up under the crossing tower in a reordering of the 1970s. To the east of the chancel arch is a coat of arms bearing the five wounds of Christ, which has above it a spitting Jew. The Clifton family traces its ancestry back to the late twelfth century and many of its members are buried here. The earliest monument is thought to be that of Sir Gervase Clifton, who died in 1391. The other late fourteenth-century effigy is to a lady of the Nevill family. Three of only fifteen surviving brasses in the county are here. These are to later generations of Cliftons: Sir Robert (died 1478), Sir Gervase (died

1491) and George (died 1587), with his wife. George's father, yet another Gervase, died only months later and he lies with his two wives on an alabaster tomb chest. George's son, named after his grandfather, inherited the title as a baby and lived until 1666. He is portrayed by a bust in the chancel. Of his seven wives the first three are commemorated by a monument of black marble and alabaster which gives a glimpse of skulls and bones in a charnel house.

Clumber: St Mary the Virgin.

The seventh Duke of Newcastle was a fervent Anglo-Catholic and commissioned G. F. Bodley to build this church, which was dedicated in 1889. No expense was spared on the stonework, white with red dressings, a red crossing tower and darker spire, nor on the furnishings. There is much elaborate wood-carving on the choirstalls, rood and screen, font and confessional, and the stained glass is by Kempe. Seen at a distance, mirrored in the lake, the church is unforgettable.

East Markham: St John the Baptist.

This is a grand fifteenth-century church, spacious, light and obviously built by better than average craftsmen. All the proportions are right and the decoration is tasteful. The only earlier part of the church is the four-teenth-century chancel arch. Since this was the demarcation line of responsibilities — the clergy paid for the upkeep of the chancel and the parishioners for everything west of it — it is not surprising that neither wished to spend money rebuilding it. The curious base of the font is probably of the same date. The bowl is dated 1686 with a contemporary wooden cover. The pulpit, altar rails and almsbox may be slightly earlier. There is some interesting glass in the church: two female saints, fif-teenth-century, in the south aisle, and four-teenth-century heraldic roundels incorporated in the east window by Sir Ninian Comper, who also designed the altar. The medieval altar slab in the north aisle was uncovered as a result of a dream that came to a vicar at the end of the nineteenth century. There are two monuments of note: a very fine brass to Millicent Meryng, who died in 1419, and a

tomb chest to her husband, Sir John Markham (died 1409), the judge who drew up the documents for deposing Richard II. This is covered in names scratched on the surface — one as early as 1647 — and a nine men's morris and similar games.

Egmanton: St Mary.

The shrine of Our Lady of Egmanton was a centre of pilgrimage in the middle ages and the cult was revived in 1896 by the seventh Duke of Newcastle. He chose Sir Ninian Comper to refurbish this modest medieval church and restore its former glory. The exterior gives no hint of the lavish interior, with its beautifully carved rood screen, pulpit and organ case, each in glowing colours. In the chancel are the canopied statue of Our Lady, the striking high altar and bright east window, all of which are Comper's work. Some of the ancient fittings survive, notably a plain, solid Norman font and an altar table of 1685, still in the early seventeenth-century style. In the south transept there are stained glass figures of St Michael and St George dating from about 1360.

Fledborough: St Gregory.

The church goes back to Norman times, and the lower part of the tower is of this period. The upper part is thirteenth-century, as are the aisles and nave, with a clerestory added in the following century. The chancel was rebuilt in 1890 but contains an Easter sepulchre. Unlike that at Hawton (page 66), this is incomplete, with only two panels — one of three sleeping soldiers and the other of Christ rising, with angels. The main attraction is the fourteenth-century stained glass, especially in the east window of the north aisle, depicting St John the Baptist, St Andrew, the Virgin and Child, and a knight. There is more in the chancel: two saints and several heraldic shields. Also fourteenth-century are two monuments, one of a lady and the other a demi-figure of a knight. An earlier coffin slab is carved with an ornate foliate cross. The pillar almsbox invites the passer-by to 'Remember the Poore'. An eighteenth-century rector of Fledborough, the Reverend Swete-apple, is still remembered for setting up in

The Queen's Sconce, Newark (see page 60).

Blyth church (see page 63).

competition to Gretna Green in performing marriages for eloping couples with no questions asked.

Gedling: All Hallows.

The most striking aspect of this church is its tower and bulging broach spire, with dormer windows and niches, all built early in the fourteenth century. This is unusual in that it is built to the west of the north aisle, giving scope for a decorative nave window with a niche at either side at the west end. The rest of the church is mainly thirteenth-century, though the south porch and clerestory are fifteenth-century. In the chancel are a double aumbry, sedilia and piscina, and a rather crude monument to a priest, possibly fourteenth-century, judging from the fact that his hands are not held together in prayer, but crossed downwards on his body. A coffin slab with the face and feet of another priest lies near the tower. The pulpit is made up from various Elizabethan panels. There are five splendid hatchments to members of the Stanhope family and a fine eighteenth-century chandelier hangs in the nave.

Hawton: All Saints.

Although the earliest surviving parts of the church are the late thirteenth-century nave and north aisle, probably built by Sir Robert de Compton, it is the chancel, built either by his son or grandson, both called Robert, that is the finest element. The east window catches the eye first, with its magnificent tracery. On the south side is a triple sedilia with the most ornate canopy, which is a mass of foliage and saints, together with a pelican in its piety and two men picking grapes. Just east of this is an equally elaborate double piscina. On the north wall is a yet more stunning composition of three parts: first the north door, and then the founder's tomb, both with crocketed arches. The second Sir Robert died in 1330 and his rather battered effigy lies here. The third part is the Easter sepulchre. A number of these were built around this time as part of the Easter celebrations. The reserved sacrament from mass on Maundy Thursday was placed here and a vigil kept until Easter morning, when it was moved to the high altar to sym-

bolise the Resurrection. The Hawton sepulchre is in three stages. The central section is recessed and has mutilated carvings of the risen Christ, the three Marys and two angels. Below are three sleeping knights, meant to be guarding the tomb, and above is a panel of the Ascension, with Christ's feet disappearing into the clouds, watched by the twelve disciples. Less well-preserved sepulchres may be seen at Arnold, Fledborough (page 64), Sibthorpe and several Lincolnshire churches. The chancel screen is late fifteenth-century, as are the clerestory and the tower, built by Sir Thomas Molyneux, whose arms appear on the doorway.

Holme by Newark: St Giles.

Although the north wall of the church and the low tower with its broach spire were built around 1300, the church as it now stands is largely a rebuilding of 1485. John Barton, originally from Lancashire, made his fortune as a wool merchant. The south aisle and Lady Chapel are entirely due to his generosity. He died in 1491 and his effigy lies, together with that of his wife Isabella, on a table tomb, with a cadaver beneath, between the chancel and the Lady Chapel. The roof corbels display his merchant's mark and the arms of the Staple of Calais, through which he traded. A relative, Robert Barton, added the porch in about 1550. The room above is known as Nan Scott's Chamber after a woman who took refuge in it from the plague that was raging in 1666 and refused to come out again, even when the plague had abated. There is interesting woodwork in the church, notably the bench ends of 1485, the fifteenth-century screen and seventeenth-century altar rails. The pulpit and tower screen were made up from old panels in the very sympathetic restoration carried out in the 1930s, when ancient glass was put into the east window. Some of it originally belonged to the church, but the four quatrefoils came from the ruined church at Annesley, and other pieces from Salisbury and Beauvais.

Langar: St Andrew.

Although the church was built in the thirteenth century it was very heavily restored in the 1860s by the Reverend Thomas Butler, father of the novelist Samuel Butler (page 108). It is of cruciform design, with a central crossing tower. The transepts contain a number of interesting monuments. The earliest is an inscription to George Chaworth, who died in 1521. His son John (died 1558) lies on a tomb chest with his wife, mourned by his children, one of whom, George, is represented by another effigy in full armour, erected at the time of his death in 1587. Far surpassing these in grandeur is the tomb of Thomas, Lord Scroope, and his wife Philadelphia. They lie resplendent under a heavy canopy with their coat of arms at each corner. Kneeling at their feet is their son Emmanuel, who spared no expense in raising this monument on his father's death in 1609. There are two busts to the first and second Viscounts Howe, but the most famous of the family, Richard, third Viscount and first Earl Howe, has only a plain tablet. He was the admiral who defeated the French off Ushant on 1st June 1794. An Italian sixteenth-century altar cloth, part of his booty, hangs on the wall. Other fittings include a fifteenth-century font, a Jacobean pulpit and reading desk and baluster altar rails of 1635.

Newark: St Mary Magdalen.

This is the finest parish church in Nottinghamshire, its spire visible from a long way off, dominating the town. The early twelfth-century crypt, which now houses the treasury, is the oldest surviving part of the church. About a century later the lower stages of the tower were erected (the large window over the west door that so unbalances the composition is not original). Another century later the ornate top storey and spire were added, and the south aisle was built. Not until the middle of the fifteenth century did work begin again, when the nave and north aisle were rebuilt, followed by the chancel and its aisles, and finally, in the early sixteenth century, the transepts. The exterior is fascinating, with a wealth of carvings and flowing tracery.

The interior of the church is no less splendid. There is much stained glass, notably of the fourteenth and fifteenth centuries in the east window of the south chapel, though the

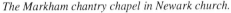

The Markham chantry chapel in Newark church.

main east window by Hardman and that in the nave by Gerente of Paris are particularly good nineteenth-century work. Of the many monuments, one of the best was brought here from Cotham church and commemorates Anne Markham (died 1601) with her seven children. Another is by Roubiliac — a portrait of Anne Taylor (1757). The most important brass in the county is here. It is one of only a dozen Flemish-made brasses in England, and one of the largest, depicting Alan Fleming (died 1363), surrounded by a variety of saints. The woodwork, too, is excellent: a screen of 1508 made by Thomas Drawswerd of York, and slightly later choirstalls with 26 misericords, including a dragon, an owl and a green man. Either side of the chancel are two chantry chapels, that on the north founded by Thomas Meyring in 1500 and that on the south by Robert Markham in 1508. This retains two painted panels from a Dance of Death, one of a skeleton and the other of a fashionably dressed nobleman. The fifteenth-century font, with saints around the base, was damaged in the Civil War; the heads of the saints and the bowl were replaced at the Restoration. The reredos behind the high altar is by Sir Ninian Comper, whose work may also be seen at Egmanton (page 64). Finally the treasury should not be missed, as some of the church's magnificent plate is displayed here, along with items on loan from other parishes in the diocese.

Nottingham: St Mary.

This is the largest parish church in Nottingham, and probably the oldest, since it appears to have been founded in Saxon times. It is the civic church and during the major periods of the city's prosperity much money was spent on it. The present building dates largely from the fifteenth century, with nineteenth- and early twentieth-century additions. It is built on a cruciform pattern with nave, aisles, transepts, chancel and a central crossing tower in finest Perpendicular style. The height of the church is emphasised by the tall windows, those at each end of the transepts being particularly large. There is stained glass by most of the best nineteenth-century makers — Hardman, Ward & Hughes, Burlisson &

Grylls, Clayton & Bell, Heaton, Butler & Bayne and Kempe. Only a few fragments of the original glass survive in the south chapel. The south porch, with elaborate archway and panelling, is attractively weatherbeaten, and the bronze doors, early twentieth-century, have scenes from the life of Christ and the Virgin Mary, with a notable Pietà. The woodwork, apart from the Jacobean altar table in the north transept, is of the 1870s and 1880s. The original choirstalls with misericords were given to the church of St Stephen, Sneinton. The Bishop's throne was carved in 1890, when the chapter house was also built, in the expectation that St Mary would become the cathedral of the diocese of Southwell. Other items of interest are the fifteenth-century font, the lion and the unicorn with the royal arms and the arms of Nottingham from the early eighteenth century, and the organ by Marcussen, the noted Danish maker (1973). The fifteenth-century monuments are rather the worse for wear, but there is a Nottingham alabaster panel depicting St Thomas à Becket. There is a variety of memorial tablets, a number of which are to members of the Plumptre family. Henry Plumptre, who died in 1719, aged ten, was, according to the inscription, something of an infant prodigy.

Ossington: Holy Rood.

The medieval church was demolished in 1782 by Robert Denison, who had just inherited the Hall from his brother, William. He employed John Carr, an architect from York, to erect the present church in the currently fashionable classical style. The three-stage tower is topped by a cupola. Externally the nave and chancel are all under one hipped roof and, viewed from the south, symmetrical with two round-headed windows either side of the entrance portico. Internally the chancel is separated from the nave by three arches. The altar painting of Christ at the pool of Siloam is Italian, seventeenth-century. At the west end are monuments to both the Denison brothers (Robert outlived his brother by only three years and may have intended the church to be a tribute to William). These fine statues are by Nollekens. William was a self-made man, and on the plinth are carved a ship with

St Nicholas church, Nottingham (see page 30).

bales of wool on the quay and sheep grazing. He bought the ancestors along with the Hall (itself demolished in 1963) and Robert respected their tombs when rebuilding the church. The brass on the south side is to Reynolde Peckham (died 1551) and his wife Elizabeth. This is a palimpsest, incised on the back of earlier memorials, the figures being cut from a fourteenth-century Flemish brass, and the inscription from sixteenth-century brasses. On the north is an imposing monument erected in 1602 to William and Grace Cartwright, who kneel facing each other, with their six sons and six daughters below.

Papplewick: St James.

The tower is fourteenth-century, but the rest of the church was demolished and rebuilt in a fanciful Gothick style in 1795. That date is inscribed on the porch, along with the initials FM, for Frederick Montagu, who paid for all the work. Not all the old church was destroyed: four cross-slabs are built into the porch and doorway, two with bellows, commemorating ironworkers, one with a horn, bow and arrow for a forester and one with a billhook for a woodward. Also in the porch are two figures, probably both representing St James. Inside, the church is very narrow — only 15 feet (4.5 metres) wide. To accommodate everybody, a gallery was built along the west and north walls. At the eastern end of this is the squire's pew with fireplace and hat pegs. The royal arms hang on the west wall. There are two fonts: a small marble basin on a wooden column, put in the church at the rebuilding, and the original thirteenth-century one. The glass in the westernmost window on the south side is fifteenth-century, with St Peter, St Stephen, a kneeling knight and six monks. The east window, depicting Faith and Hope, was based by Francis Eginton on Sir Joshua Reynolds's window in New College chapel, Oxford.

Ratcliffe on Soar: Holy Trinity.

The church is mainly thirteenth- and fourteenth-century, but successive generations have left their mark, notably in the Georgian windows of the north aisle and the general restoration of 1891. One of the fonts, although

Victorian, was not part of this restoration but came from Kingston on Soar. The original font is fourteenth-century with a cover of about 1660. In 1891 the medieval stone altar slab was discovered and re-erected in the chancel, with the seventeenth-century communion table being moved to the south aisle. The altar rails of 1638 were left *in situ*. There are eleven incised slabs, unfortunately none in good condition, dating from the last quarter of the fifteenth century to the first quarter of the sixteenth. However, four later Tudor and Stuart monuments are particularly fine. Ralph Sacheverell (died 1539) lies alongside his first wife Cecily, on a tomb chest under a niche in the north chapel. His son, Henry (died 1558), lies nearby on another tomb chest, with his wife Lucy; their seventeen children are carved along the sides. The next Henry Sacheverell (died 1586) and his wife Jane have a similar monument, but the third Henry (died 1626) has a more elaborate arrangement. Rather than have a particularly large tomb chest to accommodate him and his three wives, he lies in state alone, with his three wives kneeling on a wall monument above him; this is surmounted by his coat of arms. All the Sacheverell knights are in armour and their ladies fashionably dressed. The alabaster effigies, although provincial work, are well carved and retain much of the original colouring. Monuments to other members of the family may be seen in the church at Barton in Fabis.

Southwell Minster: St Mary the Virgin.

As befits the cathedral church of the diocese of Southwell, this is probably the finest, largest and most ancient church in Nottinghamshire. It is built on the site of a Roman villa, but the first documentary evidence suggests that Oskytel, Archbishop of York, founded, or perhaps re-established, a church here in 956. It was never monastic and seems to have been a pro-cathedral of the Archbishops. It was certainly regarded as the mother church of the county early in the twelfth century and, even though in 1171 the Chapter of Prebendaries, or canons, was granted privileges which made it answerable only to the Pope, in practice the Archbishops did not lessen their grip on it. With short lapses under Edward VI and during the Commonwealth, it retained its status until 1840 when the appointment of Prebendaries ceased and it was demoted to being a parish church. In 1884, however, it became the cathedral of the newly formed diocese of Southwell (which until 1927 included Derbyshire as well as Nottinghamshire).

The early Norman tympanum of St Michael and the dragon and David and the lion, now in the north transept, is the oldest surviving feature. The present building was started in 1108, presumably with the east end, so it was probably about 1130 that the transepts and nave were erected in Mansfield stone. The solid Norman pillars and rounded arches of the nave, with triforium and clerestory above, give an impression of stability, as do the twin towers at the west front, completed a few years after 1150. The pyramidal steeples were reinstated in 1880, having been altered several times in previous centuries. The west porch and its doors are original but the huge west window, letting more light into the nave, which would otherwise have been rather dark, is fifteenth century.

The Norman east end was demolished and a new one, twice as long, built between 1234 and 1241. This is in a much lighter, Early English style, but like the nave it has only quite modest carving. The multiple columns and the ribs of the vaulted roof more than compensate for that and the chancel is an appropriate contrast to the rather serious nave. There are biblical scenes carved high on the Norman capitals of the crossing but the best-known of Southwell's carvings are in the chapter house. This splendid octagonal meeting place for the Prebendaries was built around 1288. It has a vaulted roof, without a central pillar for support, and is entered by a delicate double arch flanked by Purbeck marble columns, the only use of this material in the Minster. Although there are carvings of human heads, domestic animals and mythical creatures here, it is the naturalistic foliage on every available capital, spandrel and boss that is the glory of this delightful chamber.

Equally fine in its own way is the pulpitum or stone screen, dividing the nave from the choir, on which the organ now perches. This was built some thirty to fifty years after the chapter house and is much more lavish,

The Norman arcade in the north porch of Southwell Minster.

though less naturalistic, in its carving. The five-seated sedilia in the chancel are of a similar date and like the pulpitum were over-restored in 1820.

There have been no substantial additions or alterations since the fifteenth century. The Minster survived the Reformation but was damaged by Scottish troops in the Civil War. Repairs were carried out in the time of Charles II and again after a severe fire in 1711. Two major restorations were carried out: one early in the nineteenth century by Richard Ingleman, who designed some of the public buildings in Southwell, and one in 1880 by Ewan Christian.

There is some interesting woodwork, notably the six fourteenth-century misericords on the east side of the pulpitum and the fif-teenth-century 'bread pews' in the south transept. The Virgin and Child nearby was carved in 1952 for the monks at Kelham and was given to the Minster by them when they left there in 1974. The rest dates from Southwell's early years as a cathedral. The font, made by William Balme of Mansfield in 1661, replaces one destroyed in the Civil War. There are only two important monuments: a superb ala-baster effigy of Archbishop Sandys (died 1558) and the kneeling bronze figure of Bishop Ridding (died 1904). Much of the stained glass is Victorian by Kempe, O'Connor and Clayton & Bell, but there is some medieval English and later Flemish glass in the chapter house. The best by far is the sixteenth-century French glass in the lower east window, which came from the Temple church in Paris. Not to be missed, either, is the early sixteenth-century brass eagle lectern which was dredged up from the lake at Newstead.

Strelley: All Saints.

Of the earliest stone church only the thir-teenth-century base of the tower remains, the rest having been built in Mansfield stone through the generosity of Sir Sampson de Strelley in the second half of the fourteenth century, with the clerestory being added in the following century. It consists of a nave, north and south aisles and transepts, and a large chancel which houses the founder's tomb. Although he died in 1390, his wife Elizabeth lived another fifteen years and the monument may have been erected at her death. The fine alabaster effigies depict the couple holding hands. There is a good incised slab to John de Strelley (died 1421); three more incised slabs to other members of the family are now rather worn. Robert de Strelley (died 1487) and his wife are commemorated by a brass. John de Strelley (died 1501) and his wife Sanchia lie on a magnificent tomb chest in a heavily carved niche in the north wall of the chancel. The canopy shows Abraham, with souls in his bosom, St John Baptist and St John the Evangelist. The knight's head rests on a helm with the crest of a Saracen's head and at his feet are a fine lion and two tiny figures telling their beads and mourning his death. The fifteenth-century rood screen is exceptionally tall and slender and in remarkably good condition. Not surprisingly the figures above are twentieth-century. Two of the fifteenth-century choirstalls have rather crude misericords: a bishop raising his hand in blessing and a grotesque naked figure. Part of the pulpit is of the same date but the back and sounding board are Jacobean. There is some Flemish glass in the church: St Bartholomew and St Ugbert (both fourteenth-century) and St James (sixteenth century) in the nave and a variety of eighteenth-century work in the east win-dow of the south chapel.

Teversal: St Catherine.

The Norman south doorway may once have been sited at the west end until the tower was built in the fifteenth century. It has a number of motifs: a dove, a lamb, three fishes and crosses and the figure of a priest. The door itself is medieval. The aisles with their squat pillars are thirteenth-century. It is the interior of the church which is of greatest interest as it was refitted in the seventeenth century with a squire's pew with canopy, christening pew, box pews, communion table, altar rails, two-decker pulpit and west gallery. The roof and a number of windows were also renewed then. The Molyneux family were lords of the manor at that time. Sir Francis (died 1674) is com-memorated by an undistinguished bust. Sir

The east window of the Lace Hall, formerly the Unitarian chapel, High Pavement, Nottingham (see page 92).

Thurgarton Priory.

John (died 1691) and his wife Lucy have a far superior monument with their busts under an elaborate pediment, and their son Francis (died 1741) and his wife have a similar but slightly more modest memorial. A later Sir Francis (died 1812) has his likeness in profile on a medallion surrounded by the Garter, as befitted a Gentleman Usher of the Black Rod. Two earlier owners of Teversal have incised slabs in the south aisle: Roger Greenhalgh (died 1563) and Ann, his wife (died 1538). There are eight Molyneux hatchments, the latest being as recent as 1876. The royal arms are eighteenth-century.

Thurgarton Priory: St Peter.

The priory was founded by Ralph Deyncourt between 1119 and 1139 but was largely dismantled after the Dissolution by William Cooper, cup-bearer to Henry VIII, who used the materials to build himself a mansion south of the church. This was in its turn demolished by his descendant John Gilbert Cooper, who built a new house in 1777 over the undercroft of the medieval cloisters. The Augustinian monks must have had wealthy patrons as in its heyday the church seems to have been as large as Southwell Minster. What is left dates from about 1230 and consists of the west front, three bays of the nave and the north tower, which originally had a counterpart to the south. Although incomplete, it is still impressive. The north aisle and chancel were added in 1852 to a design by the Nottingham architect T. C. Hine. The chancel incorporates a fine Decorated window with bracket and canopy of about 1330. Three stalls with their misericords presumably came from the monks' choir. The medieval altar slab was found down a well and is now restored to its original use. Walter Hilton, author of the fourteenth-century spiritual classic *The Ladder of Perfection*, was a canon of this priory.

Whatton: St John of Beverley.

The church dates from Norman times, as can be seen from the north arch of the central tower, but was largely rebuilt in the fourteenth century. The nave and the north aisle with its two beautifully carved corbels of King David and an angel musician date from this period. The rest is the result of nineteenth-century restorations, notably the tower, which was almost entirely rebuilt under the direction of Thomas Butler, rector of Langar, in 1870. The stained glass was installed later in the century with windows by Heaton, Butler & Bayne, Kempe, and best of all by Morris & Company to designs by Burne-Jones. The font is dated 1662 and is one of a number, including that in Southwell Minster, erected just after the Restoration to replace those damaged under the Commonwealth. There are three fourteenth-century effigies, a priest and two knights, and an incised slab to Thomas Cranmer, senior, who died in 1501.

Willoughby on the Wolds: St Mary and All Saints.

This is the last resting place of several generations of the Willoughby family, who took the name of their estate in preference to their original surname of Bugge. There are worn stone effigies to two ladies of about 1300 and of Sir Richard Willoughby (died 1325) and his wife. A later Sir Richard (died 1362) lies resplendent in his judge's robes and his son, also Richard, is depicted in armour. Sir Hugh (died 1448) and his wife have the most splendid tomb in the side chapel, with finely carved panels of the Trinity and the Virgin and Child at each end, which fortunately escaped being defaced in the following centuries. Sir Hugh's descendants are buried at Wollaton (see below). Also buried in the church was Colonel Michael Stanhope, whose brass tablet says that he 'was slayne in Willoughby Field in the month of July 1648 in the 24 yeare of his age being a souldier for King Charles the First'. This was one of the last skirmishes of the Civil War, fought near the Fosse Way.

The church itself has a thirteenth-century nave with fifteenth-century clerestory, and fourteenth-century aisles, tower and broach spire. The large chancel was rebuilt in 1891. The font dates from about 1340 and there are some later fourteenth-century floor tiles.

Wollaton: St Leonard.

The church is mainly fourteenth-century and has a notable tower, with open arches, since glazed, to allow processions to pass through. The north aisle was rebuilt about 1500 and the south aisle dates from the general restoration of 1885. Fortunately, since such items were not always to their taste, the Victorians retained the magnificent classical reredos, with its Corinthian columns, at the east end. This was erected about 1660. There are several Willoughby monuments here, continuing the series of earlier tombs at Willoughby on the Wolds (see above). The first, dated 1471, is a fine brass to Richard and Anne, which is set on a low altar tomb, with one side unenclosed to display a stone corpse under the slab. The same gruesome reminder of man's mortality can be seen

through the arches of the altar tomb of Sir Henry (died 1528), who lies above, beside his four wives, each carved half-size. Later, more modest monuments to the family are by Bacon and Westmacott. Also commemorated here is Robert Smythson (died 1614), 'Architector and Survayor unto the most worthy house of Wollaton and diverse others of great account'. The stained glass is mainly twentieth-century — late work by Kempe, two windows by Christopher Whall and the most recent by Hardman.

Worksop: Priory Church of St Cuthbert and St Mary.

The Augustinian priory was founded in 1103 by William de Lovetot, but the present nave, the western front and its towers, apart from the battlements, date from the second half of the twelfth century. The heavy ironbound door in the south porch is of this period, although the porch itself is thirteenth-century. Also thirteenth-century was the eastern part of the church, nearly twice as long as the nave, but all of this was demolished at the Dissolution, except for the Lady Chapel, which was left roofless. The nave, being the parish church, was retained but not until the twentieth century was much more work done. In the 1920s and 1930s the chapel was restored and north and south transepts built, partly from the original stone that had been reused for a farm and mill nearly four centuries earlier. The east end was built in a more modern style in the late 1960s: opinion is divided as to how suitable this addition is.

The Norman nave is quite high, with its triforium and clerestory, and the arches and capitals are rather monotonously decorated. The Lady Chapel is a complete contrast, being lighter and plainer. In the south transept are a Jacobean communion table and three rather battered monuments to Sir Thomas Neville (died 1406), his wife Joan (1395) and her brother Lord Furnival (1366). A further *memento mori* is in the north aisle — a skull with an arrow head still embedded in it.

Langar Rectory was the birthplace of Samuel Butler (see page 108).

The interior of a framework knitter's cottage at Ruddington (see page 94).

The reconstruction of a lacemaker's cottage is displayed at 'The Story of Nottingham Lace' (see page 92).

The tableau 'Adventure at the Mill' from The Tales of Robin Hood (see page 105).

6
Historic buildings and gardens

Hodsock Priory Gardens, Blyth, Worksop S81 0TY. Telephone: 0909 591204.
Open Sunday and Monday at Bank Holidays, also certain weekdays in summer. Teas.

There was never a priory at Hodsock. The present house, which is not open to the public, is nineteenth-century but the dry moat of an earlier manor must still be crossed to reach it. The fine brick-built Tudor gatehouse guarding it is a Grade I listed building. The moat banks enclose the noted 5 acre (2 hectare) garden. There are mature trees including cornus, Indian bean, swamp cypress and tulip tree, and established ilex and beech hedges. Mixed borders are planted for year-round colour. Other features are a small lake, a bog garden and rose garden, but Hodsock is perhaps best known for its spectacular snowdrops in the garden and wood.

Holme Pierrepont Hall, Holme Pierrepont, Nottingham NG12 2LD. Telephone: 0602 332371.
Open, afternoons only, Sundays in June; Thursdays and Sundays in July; Thursdays, Fridays and Sundays in August; and also Sunday to Tuesday at Easter, Spring and Summer Bank Holidays. Teas.

The Pierreponts acquired Holme in 1284 when Sir Henry married Annora Manvers and the property remains in the hands of their descendants. The present house was built early in the sixteenth century, one of the first instances of brick building in the county. It is low, only two storeys high, with a third storey to each of the two towers either side of the main south entrance. The eastern range is of a similar age, but the northern is nineteenth-century. At one time this wing was much grander, built by Robert Pierrepont, first Earl of Kingston, in 1628 but demolished a hundred years or so later.

Inside, the rooms to the left of the entrance, which were lodgings for retainers, have been restored to their original state and furnished with mainly seventeenth-century furniture. In one of the bedrooms on this wing the ceiling has been removed to reveal the impressive roof construction. On the first floor of the eastern range is the Long Gallery, in which some of the chequered building history can be seen. At the end of the Long Gallery is the finely carved Grand Staircase, dating from the time of Charles II and installed here when the northern wing was pulled down. The house contains some good Georgian furniture and many family portraits. The courtyard garden was laid out in 1875 and nearly a century later the east garden was planted. Jacob sheep roam in the park.

The church next to the house is also worth a visit. The tower and spire are fifteenth-century and the exterior of the body of the church, which is classical with a touch of Gothic to it, was built in 1666. Inside, however, the pillars are thirteenth-century. The chancel was rebuilt by T. C. Hine of Nottingham in 1878. The Pierrepont monuments are interesting, notably the brass to an unknown lady of about 1385, the alabaster effigy of Sir Henry Pierrepont (died 1499) and that of a later Sir Henry (died 1615). Two early nineteenth-century memorials are by Flaxman.

Newstead Abbey, Linby, Nottingham NG15 8GE. Telephone: 0623 793557. City of Nottingham.
Grounds open all year. House open daily April to September. Café and restaurant.

Newstead was an Augustinian priory, founded by Henry II in about 1170. Most of the medieval remains date from a major rebuilding about a century later. The west front is particularly fine. The central window has gone, but the delicate tracery in the blank windows either side is most attractive. Surprisingly, statues of Christ, above the main entrance, and the Virgin and Child, in the gable, are still *in situ*. The rest of the church was destroyed in 1539 when Sir John Byron

The west front of Newstead Abbey and (below) the memorial to Byron's dog, Boatswain, in the gardens.

bought the property, converting the monastic quarters to his own use. In the late seventeenth or early eighteenth century the southeast wing was added, but the Byrons always had financial problems. Partly because of follies like the building of mock fortifications around the lake and sailing a twenty-gun warship on it, and partly out of sheer cussedness, the fifth Lord Byron let the house and estate go to rack and ruin. He died in 1798 in the scullery, the only room not suffering from a leaking roof. His great-nephew, the poet, who succeeded him, managed to make some rooms habitable and was very fond of the house but his riotous lifestyle (see page 109) and lack of money forced him to sell it in 1817. It was bought for £94,000 by a fellow Old Harrovian, Colonel Wildman, who spent as much again on restoration. The present appearance of the house owes as much to him as to the priors and the Byrons. He added the southwest Sussex Tower with its adjoining kitchen, based on the Abbot's Kitchen at Glastonbury, Somerset, and remodelled the south front. Later owners made few alterations and in 1931 Newstead was given to the City of Nottingham.

Holme Pierrepont Hall and church (see page 78).

Wollaton Hall, Nottingham (see page 84).

The interior, too, reflects the nineteenth century. The Great Hall, which Byron used for pistol practice since it was so derelict, is now oak-panelled with a screen and minstrels' gallery. Next to it is the Prior's Parlour, with sixteenth-century carving that came from Colwick Hall. Byron used it as his dining room, and above are his dressing room, said to be haunted by a black friar, and bedroom, complete with the splendid four-poster he had as an undergraduate. The Library is full of Byron relics, including his boxing gloves, pistols and wedding ring. More of Byron's furniture may be seen — the bookcases in the East Gallery and the bed in the Edward III Room. The Henry VII Room bears no resemblance to what it was like in Byron's time but has been magnificently decorated and furnished in oriental style by the Webbs, who owned Newstead later in the nineteenth century. The Manuscript Room is again devoted to documents by or about the poet and his family. The Saloon, formerly the monks' refectory, was used by Byron for sporting activities. It is now laid out as it was in about 1840. The fine plaster ceiling dates back to 1631-3. In the south-east wing were the private apartments, one of which was Byron's study, containing more of his personal possessions, including several skulls. On the east side of the cloisters is the chapel, once the chapter house, now in Victorian splendour. The cloister court is laid out as a Mary Garden with, in the centre, a carved water conduit which probably dates back to the sixteenth century. On the west side is the undercroft, thirteenth-century like the rest of the ground floor around the cloisters. When Colwick church was closed three Byron monuments were brought here: an incised slab on a tomb chest to Sir John (died 1567) and his two wives, two effigies for his son, also Sir John (died 1604), and his wife Alice (née Strelley), and a smaller wall monument with the kneeling figures of two Sir Johns (died 1624 and 1625) and their wives. Also in the undercroft is a portrait of Byron's favourite dog, Boatswain, whose monument stands on the site of the high altar in the ruined priory church.

The grounds extend to over 300 acres (121 hectares) and the gardens are beautiful. The Webbs, so keen on things oriental, created a Japanese water garden, but there are also a rock garden and plenty of roses, irises, ferns and a yew tunnel. Water is everywhere — lakes, streams and ponds, including Eagle Pond, where the brass lectern now in Southwell Minster was found.

Norwood Park, Southwell NG25 0PF. Telephone: 0636 812762.
Open Sunday afternoons May to August, also May Bank Holidays.

The park was one of four around Southwell belonging to the Archbishops of York and it remained in their possession until 1778. A house was built here during the Commonwealth, but it was demolished and replaced by the present house in 1763. It is a pleasant three-storey brick mansion with two lower pavilions. In 1881 the connecting passages were infilled and the front door was moved to the north-west front, with some remodelling of the interior. Inside are seventeenth- and eighteenth-century family portraits and much of the furniture is Victorian. There is a fine collection of china in the hall and all sorts of toys in the nursery. The whole house has a very lived-in feel to it.

Outside are sweeping lawns, roses and a rock garden. The grounds were also laid out in the eighteenth century when the icehouse and temple were built and the lime avenue and nearby cedars planted. Some of the oaks are much older and the fish ponds may date from the time of Domesday Book, predating the twelfth-century earth bank that surrounds the original deer park. Fruit growing on a large scale began here in 1910 and there are many acres of apple and pear trees. An orchard and woodland trail has been designed to show the estate to its best advantage.

Nottingham Castle, Nottingham NG1 6EL. Telephone: 0602 483504.
Open daily except Christmas Day.

After the battle of Hastings, William the Conqueror consolidated his hold on England by building castles in important locations, one of which was Nottingham. The high rocky site overlooking the Trent lent itself naturally to fortification and the first castle was erected

The gatehouse of Nottingham Castle.

in 1068. This was presumably of standard motte and bailey design. It is assumed that the stone walls were built early in the twelfth century. During the turbulent reign of Stephen the castle changed hands several times, but when Henry II came to the throne he fortified it still further and built new living quarters. As a result, Richard I had a difficult task when in 1194 he laid siege to the castle, which was held against him by some of John's supporters. Having taken the castle, he held a council in the Great Hall that pronounced John's banishment.

Further improvements were made throughout the thirteenth century, but there is little defence against treachery. Roger Mortimer, Earl of March and lover of Queen Isabella, deposed Edward II, who was murdered at Berkeley Castle in 1327. For three years Mortimer and the Queen ruled the country in the name of the young Edward III and came to Nottingham in October 1330 for a meeting of Parliament. They stayed in the castle, but the deputy constable allowed conspirators to enter by a passage cut through the rock and Mortimer was seized, taken to London, tried

and executed. The passage known as Mortimer's Hole is regularly opened to visitors, though another, to the north-west of the castle, may be the more likely entrance. Building continued throughout the fourteenth century, not only to keep attackers out but to keep prisoners in, including King David II of Scotland, held here in 1346. It was at Nottingham that Edward IV proclaimed himself king in 1460, and his brother, later Richard III, built new state apartments and spent much of his time here after succeeding to the throne.

Thereafter it gradually fell into disrepair until Charles I raised his standard at Nottingham on 27th August 1642 at the start of the Civil War. Finding little support, he quickly moved off to Shrewsbury and the castle was held for Parliament by Colonel Hutchinson. Although it was attacked several times by the Royalists it never surrendered. It was slighted in 1651 and rendered uninhabitable. The old castle was further demolished by the first Duke of Newcastle in 1674 when he built his palace on the site. The fourth Duke was a staunch opponent of the Reform Bill and so, when the bill was thrown out by the House of

Lords, the castle, although uninhabited and practically empty, was considered fair game by the rioters who burnt and sacked it on 10th October 1831. It was left a charred ruin for 45 years, until it was rebuilt as the Midland Counties Art Museum.

It is a disappointment to tourists that so little of the medieval castle remains. The gatehouse was built in the thirteenth century but is much restored, as is the outer bailey running to the south-east of it, with the slightly later Edward's Tower halfway along. Part of the middle moat survives, between the palace and the bandstand in the outer bailey. This is crossed by the middle bridge, which replaced the drawbridge in the sixteenth century. Of the middle bailey defences only the base of the Black Tower (*c*.1270) and a section of wall leading to King Richard's Tower (*c*.1476) are left. The Dukes' palace is on the site of the upper bailey. It is in a baroque style with a number of classical features, some of which may be due to the rebuilding by T. C. Hine, who also altered the roof and reduced the original three storeys to two to admit more light. It now houses the Castle Museum (page 90), and its Italian palazzo architecture seems quite appropriate for the purpose. However, it is not the stuff of which Robin Hood legends are made.

Painters' Paradise, Patchings Farm Art Centre, Oxton Road, Calverton, Nottingham NG14 6NU. Telephone: 0602 653479.
Open daily except Christmas Day and Boxing Day. Licensed restaurant.

As the name suggests, these gardens, covering 38 acres (15.5 hectares), have been designed with artists in mind, and there are ten gazebos in which people can paint in comfort. One is intended for use by the disabled, with raised flowerbeds around it. Elements are based on Monet's garden at Giverny, with a grand allée which has pergolas of roses and honeysuckle and the famous bridge over a lake of waterlilies. There are a butterfly garden, woodland and a wildflower meadow, with several farming implements as stage props and even a grain stack that doubles as a birdwatcher's hide.

The bandstand in the outer bailey of Nottingham Castle.

Pureland Japanese Garden, North Clifton, Newark NG23 7AT. Telephone: 0777 228567.

Open Easter to October, Tuesday to Saturday afternoons, Sunday and Bank Holiday mornings and afternoons; at other times by appointment only.

In 1981 the Japanese-born monk Maitreya began the creation of this 1½ acre (0.6 hectare) garden in the grounds of the Pureland Relaxation and Meditation Centre to provide a tranquil place where students and visitors can go to find inner peace.

Wollaton Hall, Wollaton Park, Nottingham NG8 2AE. Telephone: 0602 281333 or 281130.

Open daily except Christmas Day.

From relatively humble beginnings the Willoughby family, by means of well-chosen marriages and commerce, rose to prominence. Sir Francis Willoughby (*c*.1540-96), on the strength of profits from his nearby coal mines, decided to build himself an appropriately grandiose house, though the cost of it, coupled with losses incurred in his less profitable business ventures of ironworking and growing woad, nearly bankrupted him. Work started in 1580 and lasted eight years. The architect was Robert Smythson, who lies buried in Wollaton church (page 75). He was noted for having designed Longleat, Hardwick Hall and Worksop Manor (presumably also Worksop Manor Lodge). It is built in Ancaster stone, two storeys high (three at each corner tower), with a high central tower above the Great Hall, to give it light. The façade seems rather like 'Hardwick Hall, more glass than wall'. It is smothered in decoration: classical columns, niches, busts of philosophers and mythological characters, pilasters, cartouches, strapwork, especially on the gables — flamboyant in the extreme.

Internally, however, since the building houses the Natural History Museum (page 90), only three rooms give any hint of its former grandeur. One cannot fail to be impressed by the Great Hall, 60 feet (18 metres) long by 30 feet (9 metres) wide and 50 feet (15 metres) high, with its mid seventeenth-century organ above the screen and hammerbeam style of roof. The entrance hall, by Jeffrey Wyatville, was given marble niches and at the same time, early in the nineteenth century, the room on the opposite side of the Great Hall became a salon and has been beautifully restored with period furnishings. The park was originally 802 acres (325 hectares), of which Nottingham Corporation sold 274 acres (111 hectares) for building land when it purchased the estate in 1925. The grounds are still extensive, with a golf course, lake and parkland with deer and white cattle. The outbuildings of the hall contain the Nottingham Industrial Museum (page 91). Even closer to the hall is a small icehouse. The gardens are very attractive, especially the rose garden and the flowerbeds in front of the Camellia House. This is one of the earliest cast-iron and glass buildings in England and when it was erected in 1823 by the sixth Lord Middleton it cost £10,000, which included £1400 for the camellias! A small botanic garden is open for limited periods.

7
Museums

Bestwood

Model Aviation Centre, Goosedale, Moor Road, Bestwood, Nottingham NG6 8UJ. Telephone: 0602 632175.
Open daily except Christmas Day and Boxing Day. Restaurant.

The museum has accurate models of a wide variety of aircraft at up to half the scale of the original. As well as finished models, which are used for regular flying displays, others can be seen in different stages of construction.

Cromwell

The Vina Cooke Museum of Dolls and Bygone Childhood, The Old Rectory, Cromwell, Newark NG23 6JE. Telephone: 0636 821364.
Open daily, morning and afternoon, except Christmas Day and Boxing Day; in evenings by appointment.

The Old Rectory was built around 1680 as a dower house and, with later additions, is worth visiting in its own right. However, tourists come mainly for the collection of dolls. Vina Cooke has antique and modern dolls, restores them and makes her own character dolls. There are hundreds of them, in all shapes and sizes, together with dolls' houses, prams, teddy bears, christening gowns, costumes and accessories and all sorts of toys. Facilities include a tea room and a shop.

Eastwood

D. H. Lawrence Birthplace Museum, 8a Victoria Street, Eastwood, Nottingham NG16 1AW. Telephone: 0773 763312. Broxtowe Borough Council.
Open daily except from 24th December to 1st January.

It was in this small terraced house, two up, two down and an attic, that D. H. Lawrence was born on 11th September 1885. The house has been furnished as it would have been at that time and includes a few items that be-longed to the Lawrence family. The front window is larger than usual to display the baby clothes and other linen that Mrs Lawrence sold to earn a little money besides her husband's fluctuating miner's wage. The adjoining property, now incorporated, houses new exhibition rooms, and a video presentation.

The family lived here until 1887, when they moved to 28 Garden Road, Eastwood, a more substantial end-of-terrace house. This is now known as the 'Sons and Lovers' cottage, since Lawrence used it as a model for the Morels' house, one of the terrace known as The Bottoms in that novel. It, too, is laid out as in Lawrence's time but is open only by appointment (telephone: 0773 719786). In 1891 the family moved to Walker Street, the 'third house in the street', according to Lawrence, which may be either number 8 or number 12. The last house in which he lived in Eastwood was the semi-detached 97 Lynncroft, his home from 1902 until 1908, when he left for Croydon.

Laxton

Laxton Visitor Centre, Laxton, Newark NG22 0NJ. Telephone: 0777 870376.
Open daily.

A small display sets out the importance of the unique survival of open-field farming at Laxton, with details of ancient and modern farming methods. It also covers the history of the village, including the references found in the Domesday Book, the castle and the church. The Laxton Heritage Museum, housed in a 1760 barn at Lilac Farm, has a range of farm tools and machinery and is open by appointment (telephone as above).

Mansfield

Mansfield Museum and Art Gallery, Leeming Street, Mansfield NG18 1NG. Telephone: 0623 663088.
Open daily except Sundays.

The displays in this museum concentrate to a large extent on local interest. One gallery is devoted to the natural history and geology of the area and its early history, with a model of a Roman villa that was discovered at Mansfield Woodhouse. The spacious entrance hall shows more recent history and the town's coal-mining industry in photographs and documents alongside such exhibits as a penny-farthing bicycle and rails from the Mansfield to Pinxton Railway of 1819. A gallery of fine and decorative art carries on the local theme with the watercolours of A. S. Buxton (1867-1932), who recorded views of Mansfield, including features, such as the rock houses, which have long since disappeared. The ceramics collection includes not only Wedgwood and lustreware, but a notable array of late eighteenth- and early nineteenth-century porcelain, the work of William Billingsley (1758-1828). He was probably more successful as a decorator than as a manufacturer of porcelain, and some of his most delicate designs were painted during his four years at Mansfield from 1799 to 1803.

Newark

Millgate Folk Museum, 48 Millgate, Newark NG24 4TS. Telephone: 0636 79403.
Open daily, but telephone to check weekend opening from January to March.

The river Trent was a great asset for Newark's commerce, particularly with the formation of the Trent Navigation Company in 1783 to carry out improvements. The company built a large warehouse and adjoining oilseed mill in 1870, but with the decline in river traffic in the twentieth century another use had to be found for the premises, which now house the Millgate Folk Museum. The emphasis here is on everyday life in the nineteenth and twentieth centuries. Many of the displays take the form of shops or shop-fronts including a post office, ironmonger's, cobbler's, tobacconist's, chemist's and dress shops. There are also a bar and a ticket office, and a reconstruction of the ground-floor accommodation of a terraced house of the 1900s, complete with outside toilet and coal shed. Among the exhibits are a variety of early domestic appliances from hip baths to mangles and a number of agricultural implements. The 1940s are represented by an Anderson shelter and other Second World War memorabilia. A printer works at the museum demonstrating an old yet living craft.

Newark Air Museum, The Airfield, Winthorpe, Newark NG24 2NY. Telephone: 0636 707170.
Open daily.

Winthorpe Airfield was a Second World War bomber station but was hardly used from 1945 until 1967, when the museum's first plane, a Percival Prentice, flew in. There are now forty planes, nearly half of which are displayed under cover. These range from Armstrong Whitworth Meteors to Westland Helicopters and include the only examples of a General Aircraft Monospar and a Saab 91B Safir to be found in Britain. In addition there is a variety of engines, uniforms, models and memorabilia on display.

Newark Civic Plate Collection, Newark Town Hall, Market Place, Newark NG24 1DU. Telephone: 0636 640100.
Open Monday to Friday, except Bank Holidays.

The town has a good collection of antique silver, including a large silver-gilt standing cup and a monteith with thirteen cups, both from the reign of James II. Amongst other pieces are several tankards and a Dublin-made George III soup tureen. A hoard of 97 gold coins from the early seventeenth century was discovered in 1961 and these are on display along with 99 Newark siege pieces.

Newark Museum, Appletongate, Newark NG24 1JY. Telephone: 0636 702358.
Open daily except Thursday; also closed Sundays October to March, Christmas Eve, Christmas Day, New Year's Eve and New Year's Day.

The museum was formerly the Magnus Grammar School, founded by Thomas Magnus, Archdeacon of the East Riding of Yorkshire. The original schoolroom was erected in 1529 and is now known as Tudor Hall. The school was extended in 1817, although this extension of the building does not belong to the museum. A new schoolroom was built in 1835 and this now forms the main exhibition hall. In 1909 the school moved to new premises in Newark and the museum opened in 1912.

Newark has a long and distinguished history and this is reflected in the museum. Prehistoric artefacts and bronze age swords and axeheads found locally are on display, as are Roman archaeological finds. A large Anglo-Saxon cemetery was discovered at Millgate, Newark, and some of the grave goods and burial urns are on exhibition.

The museum also displays objects from the seventeenth-century. In the uncertainty of the Civil War affluent people often buried their wealth. Two hoards of coins found in the area are on display: one of these contains 1571 silver coins, dating from Edward VI to Charles I. In the Civil War Newark was besieged three times and during the last siege coinage was in such short supply that the town minted its own diamond-shaped coins. Some examples of these coins can also be seen here.

The wooden hand press on which Byron's first volume of poems was printed is in the Newark Museum. Below is one of the smocks for which Newark was noted, now in the Millgate Folk Museum.

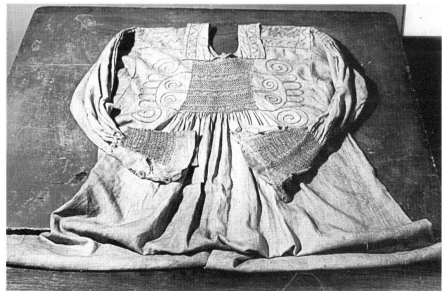

The Brewhouse Yard Museum, Nottingham.

Other exhibits include the printing press use to print Byron's first volume of poetry and militaria relating to local regiments.

Nottingham

Brewhouse Yard Museum, Castle Boulevard, Nottingham NG7 1FB. Telephone: 0602 483504, extension 3600.
Open daily except Christmas Day.

The museum is housed in a terrace of four seventeenth-century cottages at the foot of the Castle rock, together with a fifth set slightly higher and to one side. This is the museum of everyday life in Nottingham, with displays showing material up to the 1990s. There are rooms furnished as in Victorian times, a bedroom, dining room and kitchen and shop-window displays of the 1920s and 1930s — barber's, doctor's, pawnbroker's and ironmonger's shops, a music shop and one selling electrical household goods. Three larger rooms are equipped as a grocer's, a chemist's and a cobbler-cum-saddler's. Most of the exhibits have local connections, having been donated by people from the Nottingham

area. Two of the cellars, cut into the rock itself, are open, one as an ale cellar with barrels and flasks of Nottingham brewers, and another as an air-raid shelter with suitable Second World War memorabilia. Rock Cottage is set out as a schoolroom and a 1930s toy shop.

Canal Museum, Canal Street, Nottingham NG1 7EH. Telephone: 0602 598835.
Open Wednesday to Sunday, except Fridays in winter and Christmas Day.

What was once the Fellows, Morton & Clayton warehouse is now the Canal Museum. The mid-Victorian building was in use by the company, one of the largest firms of canal carriers, until it went into voluntary liquidation in 1948. (The separate office block, built in 1895, is now a pub.) The four-storey building has an archway over a basin at right angles to the canal itself, and the museum entrance is alongside. By a series of trap-doors goods could be hoisted from the barges, or flyboats as they were known, to any of the floors above. The main emphasis of the museum is on displays and models showing the history of the Trent valley and man's attempts to control the river. This includes embankments, bridges, locks (the earliest in the county was at Shelford in the sixteenth century) and the use of water from the river to cool the steam used by the generators in power stations. Seated in a mock-up of a barge, one can take an audio-visual 'Trip down the Trent'. An unusual exhibit is the Art Nouveau sideboard with a mirror above, whose frame is carved in the style of Trent Bridge. The rise and decline of the canals built to create a network of navigable waterways is given suitable prominence and includes reconstructions of a corner of the warehouse in its heyday and of a canal office.

On Sundays and Bank Holidays in summer boat trips along the Nottingham and Beeston Canal leave from the Canal Museum. They are operated by the Sherwood Line (telephone: 0530 834326).

Greens Mill and Science Centre, Windmill Lane, Sneinton, Nottingham NG2 4QB. Telephone: 0602 503635.
Open all year, Wednesday to Sunday and Bank Holiday Mondays. Closed Christmas Day.

George Green senior was a prosperous Nottingham baker who bought the old post mill at Sneinton in 1807. This he removed and built a five-storey brick tower mill in its place. Unfortunately, like so many windmills, it became derelict in the twentieth century and was badly damaged by fire in 1947, remaining in a poor state for a further thirty years or more. It was decided to restore it, although little more than the outer shell survived and completely new fittings had to be made. Nevertheless by 1986 it was back in working order and is a notable landmark on the city skyline.

An important reason behind the restoration is that George Green junior (1793-1841) worked in the mill until his father's death in 1829, when he let it out. His main claim to fame, however, is as a brilliant, largely self-taught mathematician and scientist, propounding in 1828 what is now known as Green's Theorem in his 'Essay on the Application of

Mathematical Analysis to the Theories of Electricity and Magnetism'. Almost unrecognised at the time, it has since proved to play an essential role in nuclear physics and quantum electrodynamics. New buildings have been erected next to the mill to display exhibits relating to his scientific achievements, and to the history of mills and milling in general and Greens Mill in particular.

Museum of Costume and Textiles, 51 Castle Gate, Nottingham NG1 6AF. Telephone: 0602 483504.
Open daily except Christmas Day.

This terrace of brick houses, with their fine doorways, was built by Cornelius Launder, a former High Sheriff, and his wife Mary in 1788. Fittingly, the first display in a sequence of six rooms in the museum, each with period furnishings and models wearing appropriate

Greens Mill, Sneinton, Nottingham.

clothing, is of *c.*1790. Three rooms show nine-teenth-century dress and the last two are of about 1910 and 1935. The remainder of the collection is exhibited in showcases. The most notable are the Eyre tapestries, dated 1632, with a map of the county of Nottingham, based mainly on an original print by Saxton. A display of costume accessories includes fans, bonnets, purses and bags and one room is devoted to the history of lace from needle-point and bobbin laces of the sixteenth century to Nottingham machine-made lace.

Natural History Museum, Wollaton Hall, Nottingham NG8 2AE. Telephone: 0602 281333.
Open daily except Christmas Day.

Although the grandeur of Wollaton Hall (page 84) might seem an unlikely location for a natural history museum, it is not entirely inappropriate, since one of the former owners of the house, Francis Willoughby (1635-72), was a noted naturalist. Much of his work was published posthumously but proved important in providing a scientific basis for future study. His seed collection is now in the museum. Although many of the displays consist of stuffed animals, birds and fish, they are laid out imaginatively, with an attempt to repro-duce the natural environment in which each species would be found. There is an emphasis on British wildlife such as one might expect to see in the county. Not everything is dead — there are several tanks of fish and a live colony of wood ants. The mineral gallery is parti-cularly attractive and children will enjoy the room of fossils, which not only exhibits them but also explains how they came to be pre-served.

Nottingham Castle Museum, The Castle, Nottingham NG1 6EL. Telephone: 0602 483504.
Open daily except Christmas Day.

When opened by the Prince of Wales in 1878 this was the first municipal art gallery in Britain outside London. The picture galleries are on the first floor. The collection is parti-cularly strong in Victorian paintings, especially those with romantic, historical sub-ject matter, whose titles leave little to the imagination, such as Laslett J. Pott's 'Mary Queen of Scots Led to Her Execution' and Daniel Maclise's 'Robin Hood and His Merry Men Entertaining Richard the Lionheart in Sherwood Forest'. There are also country scenes by J. F. Herring, sentimental pictures like 'In Love', by Marcus Stone, and genre paintings, notably James Hayllar's 'The Old Master', in which servants and tenants pay their last respects. Old masters include re-ligious works of the Italian and North Euro-pean schools and Le Brun's 'Hercules and Diomedes', commissioned by Cardinal Riche-lieu. Modern art is represented by L. S. Lowry, Ben Nicholson and some striking gypsy paint-ings by Dame Laura Knight, who spent her formative years in Nottingham. The short-lived Richard Parkes Bonington (1802-28), born at Arnold, has a small gallery devoted to his oils and watercolours. He spent much of his artistic life in Paris and was greatly ad-mired by his friend Delacroix.

The museum also has fine collections of silver and ceramics. Although there is a charming chinoiserie monteith of 1685, most of the silver is Georgian and for domestic use, notably tea caddies and candlesticks. Work by many of the best silversmiths is exhibited: de Lamerie, the Bateman family, Matthew Boulton and in particular Paul Storr, whose magnificent silver-gilt butter-cooler in the form of a coronet is designed more to impress than to be purely functional. Display cases of jewellery, including seventeenth-century mourning slides, and another of watches are also to be found in the silver gallery. The ceramic gallery contains a wide variety of pottery and porcelain. There is a medieval jug with knights around the rim and a many-storeyed ridge-tile chimney. Three of Not-tingham's famous saltglaze stoneware bear jugs are here, along with more delicate early Wedgwood pottery and Chelsea, Derby and Parian figurines. Other rooms house glass-ware, a small ethnography collection and a number of items excavated in 1885 from the Temple of Diana at Nemi by Lord Savile, of Rufford Abbey, including a very fine marble stele with a portrait bust of Fundilia Rufa.

Two further exhibitions are of interest to anyone who wishes to learn more of the his-

The horse gin in Nottingham Industrial Museum was used for winding miners up and down a pit shaft.

tory of the city and castle. 'Castle of Care', which is how Richard III described it, is a twenty-minute audio-visual presentation on the castle. The 'Story of Nottingham' also uses videos, as well as displays, models and items from the museum collection to trace the development of the city up to the present day.

Nottingham Industrial Museum, Courtyard Buildings, Wollaton Park, Nottingham NG8 2AE. Telephone: 0602 284602.
Open daily from April to September and Thursday, Saturday and Sunday from October to March. Closed Christmas Day.

The stable block and estate offices of Wollaton Hall (page 84) were built in 1794, mainly of red brick, with an imposing south front of stone in classical style with central portico and large clock. They now house the city's industrial museum. As befits the setting, there are two carriages in the transport collection that are nearly a century older than the building — a state carriage and a post phaeton, both made in 1698. Nottingham is famous for its cycle industry, and exhibits include boneshakers, a penny-farthing and early Raleigh and Humber models. A natural

development was the motorcycle and, although in more recent times Raleigh branched out into mopeds, it was Brough that produced quality machines in the 1920s and 1930s. It was a Brough that T. E. Lawrence (of Arabia) was riding in his fatal crash in 1935. The company also manufactured cars — there is a 1935 Brough Superior on display as well as a unique 1904 Celer motor car.

Textiles are another major industry for the county and there are a number of stocking frames and knitting and lace machines in the museum. Boots have donated several exhibits: a powder-packing machine of 1936, Hathernware jars for storage and an edge-runner mill for grinding spices. Another major employer, Players, has presented a cigarette-making machine and GPT has loaned telephones and other items tracing the development of telecommunications. Also appropriate to a factory environment are several 'clocking-in' clocks as well as much earlier tower and turret clocks.

Outside there are a horse gin of 1844 used for winding miners up and down the pit shaft and various items of street furniture, notably cast-iron boundary markers from 1850 to 1933 and a very French-looking men's urinal. Pride of place, however, must go to the Basford beam engine in its specially built glass engine house. Made in 1858 by R. & W. Hawthorn of Newcastle upon Tyne, it was in constant use until 1965 at the Basford waterworks raising water from the Bunter sandstone 110 feet (34 metres) below to Belle Vue Reservoir 155 feet (47 metres) above or Mapperley Plains 255 feet (78 metres) above. There are a variety of other steam and diesel engines and also a pair of Fowler traction engines, used for steam ploughing, together with several of their ploughs and cultivators.

The Sherwood Foresters Regimental Museum, The Castle, Nottingham NG1 6EL. Telephone: 0602 483504.
Open daily except Christmas Day.

The Regimental Collection of the Sherwood Foresters continues the castle's military connection. The regiment traces its origins back to the 45th Foot, raised in 1741, which adopted the title of the Sherwood Foresters in 1866, before combining in 1881 with the 95th Foot, raised in 1823 and known as the Derbyshire Regiment. Exhibits include a number of trophies taken in battle, including the shield and sceptre of Cetewayo, defeated in the Zulu Wars. Here is the head of Derby 1st, captured at the Siege of Kotah in 1858, the first in a long succession of rams that were the regimental mascot of the 95th Foot. There are many medals, with pride of place going to the ten Victoria Crosses. One display case is dedicated to the Nottingham flying ace of the First World War, Captain Albert Ball VC. He was still only twenty when he died in 1917, having shot down 43 enemy aircraft. A statue was erected to him in the castle grounds.

The Story of Nottingham Lace, The Lace Hall, High Pavement, Nottingham NG1 1HN. Telephone: 0602 484221.
Open daily except Christmas Day and Boxing Day. Coffee shop.

At the Restoration of the monarchy two clergy from St Mary, Nottingham, and one from St Peter were deprived of their livings and became nonconformist ministers. About 1690 they built a Presbyterian meeting house on High Pavement, which eventually became Unitarian and was replaced by the present chapel in 1876. It stands in a prominent position with an impressive spire, but its chief glory is in its stained glass. The east window, dated 1902, is by Morris & Company to designs by Burne-Jones and represents twenty virtues around a central figure of Jesus. A smaller window of David and Jonathan is by the same makers and artist. Other glass is by Kempe and Holiday.

This is the setting for the Story of Nottingham Lace. There is a ten-minute audio-visual introduction to lacemaking and the history of the lace trade before the tour commences. A reconstruction of the interior of a pillow lacemaker's cottage leads on to display boards on the machine-made lace industry, illustrated with old photographs. There are two lace machines, both in working order and used for demonstrations: a huge lace-curtain machine made by the local firm of Swift & Wass Limited in 1902, and a smaller Leavers lace machine of similar date. Original pattern books indicate the range of lace made. A variety of antique dresses and modern lingerie gives an idea of the changing fashions in lace and its use. A short video imagines Richard Birkin, the noted nineteenth-century lace dealer, inspecting the present state of the industry. Some of the thirty lace manufacturers in and around Nottingham exhibit lace here, and anything from handkerchiefs to bridal wear can be purchased. The origins of the industry are not forgotten; there is always someone demonstrating pillow lace — any visitor can try his or her hand at it — and a bobbin maker turns wooden bobbins.

Ravenshead
Longdale Craft Centre and Museum, Longdale Lane, Ravenshead NG15 9AH. Telephone: 0623 794858 or 796952.
Open daily except Christmas Day and Boxing Day. Coffee lounge and restaurant.

Not only is this a flourishing craft centre, with workshops behind a reconstruction of nineteenth-century shop-fronts, but it also houses the Gordon Brown Collection of old tools and bygones. Some are in use: for example, the printmaker works with a nine-

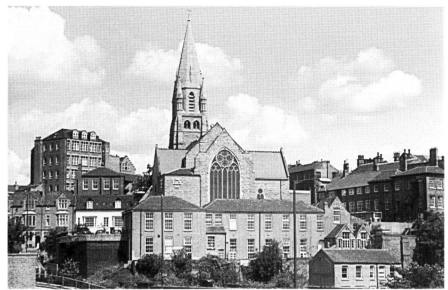

The former Unitarian chapel that houses 'The Story of Nottingham Lace' and (right) the lace-curtain machine being installed in it.

teenth-century Albion printing press and the silversmith works at a bench rescued from the Birmingham jewellery quarter. There is a wide variety not only of agricultural implements but also of tools used for thatching, plumbing and leadwork, saddlery, joinery, barrel-making and, not least, those in daily use by Mr Brown himself for woodcarving. Such items as the unique spoke-tanging and felloe-boring machine and the barrel-shaped washing machine of 1912 have, however, lain idle for many years.

Retford

Bassetlaw Museum, Amcott House, 40 Grove Street, Retford DN22 6JU. Telephone: 0777 706741. Bassetlaw District Council. *Open daily except Sunday and Bank Holiday Mondays.*

Originally a private residence built in the mid eighteenth century, Amcott House was subsequently used as council offices but has now been converted into a museum and its interior with fine plaster ceilings has been elegantly restored. A former owner and local

Upton Hall is the home of the British Horological Institute.

worthy was Stephen Pegler, who was also an amateur artist and photographer, many of whose historic photographs of the locality are in the museum collection. It contains a variety of eighteenth- and nineteenth-century glassware, pottery and porcelain, including some Chinese items and one of the saltglaze stoneware bear jugs for which Nottingham was noted. There are local archaeological finds: bronze age pottery beakers from Clumber Park; coins, pottery and domestic objects from Littleborough (Roman *Segelocum*); and a Roman gold ring with glass intaglio from Styrrup. Amongst more recent exhibits are a number of agricultural implements, household utensils, an early boneshaker and children's toys. On display also are the borough weights and measures, the borough seal, the town crier's handbell and the town clerk's wig.

Ruddington

Ruddington Framework Knitters' Museum, Chapel Street, Ruddington, Nottingham NG11 6HE. Telephone: 0602 846914.
Open Tuesday to Saturday from April to December, and Bank Holiday Mondays.

As in many villages around Nottingham, framework knitting was the major industry here; indeed in the mid nineteenth century two-thirds of the population were connected with the trade. The cottages and two small workshops were built in 1829, but the latter were replaced in the 1870s by the present ones, each capable of housing fifty frames. The two-storey brick workshops, with their long windows on each floor, are an indication of the scale of the industry, compared with that in other villages, such as Calverton and Stapleford (pages 97 and 102), where the frames generally occupied one room in a worker's cottage.

The museum has 25 knitting frames, most in working order, and regular demonstrations are given, with finished products on sale. There are also a collection of circular sock-knitting machines and an exhibition showing the development of framework knitting in the East Midlands in general and its importance to Ruddington in particular. The cottages have been furnished as they would have been for a framework knitter's family in 1850 and a hosier's family in 1900.

Ruddington Village Museum, St Peter's Rooms, Church Street, Ruddington, Nottingham NG11 6HD. Telephone: 0602 211545. *Open Easter to late October in the afternoon on Sundays and certain weekdays; every afternoon in July and August except Mondays.*

The former village school of 1852 is the setting for this museum, which concentrates on everyday life in the village. There are reconstructions of an Edwardian fish and chip shop, pharmacist's, cobbler's, ironmonger's and toy shops. Appropriately, one room is furnished as a schoolroom. An array of farm implements completes the collection.

Upton

British Horological Institute, Upton Hall, Upton, Newark NG23 5TE. Telephone: 0636 813795.
Open on Sundays in the summer.

Although a fragment of the seventeenth-century building remains, Upton Hall was largely rebuilt in a classical style in 1828, with an imposing Greek portico. The west wing was added in 1895, when the interior was remodelled, with fine plasterwork and impressive overmantels to the fireplaces. It is now the headquarters of the British Horological Institute and its fascinating collection of timepieces. As well as antique long-case and bracket clocks and more delicate watches, there are such curiosities as water clocks, a Chinese fire clock, Japanese wall clocks, a rolling ball clock and an inclined plane clock. More modern exhibits include Captain Scott's alarm watch, which he wore on his fatal Antarctic expedition in 1912, a Donald Duck pocket watch of about 1935, several British Telecom speaking clocks and a clock made entirely of wood and another of plastic.

West Stockwith

Miniature World Museum, Beechfield House, Main Street, West Stockwith, Doncaster DN10 4EY. Telephone: 0427 890982. *Open Wednesday to Sunday and Bank Holidays. Closed January. Teashop.*

This museum houses Nita Hardy's collection of over six hundred dolls, ranging from mid eighteenth-century wooden ones and Victorian wax and bisque rarities to modern plastic items. There are some forty dolls' houses as well, which children are encouraged to open, and several very detailed shops and street scenes painstakingly created by Mrs Hardy herself.

Worksop

Worksop Museum, Memorial Avenue, Worksop S80 2BP. Telephone: 0909 501148. Bassetlaw District Council.
Open daily except Sundays and Bank Holidays. Closed Thursday and Saturday afternoons.

The centrepiece of the museum is a display on 'The Pilgrim Fathers' Story', told in a sequence of panels, with appropriate illustrations, from their origins in Nottinghamshire to the foundation of their colony in America. A tableau reconstructs life below decks on the *Mayflower*. Other exhibits are of local interest, notably a wheelbarrow with silver-plated fittings and a matching ceremonial spade, used to cut the first sod for the Worksop Water Works in 1877.

8
Industrial archaeology

Anglo-Scotian Mills, Wollaton Road, Beeston (OS 129: SK 527370).

This factory was built in the 1870s for Frank Wilkinson, a major manufacturer of lace curtains. A sideline in Shetland wool hosiery accounts for the second part of the name. It is a fanciful four-storeyed building in red brick, with lancet windows, turrets and battlements, though it did not acquire this façade until after a severe fire in 1892.

An earlier silk mill, on the corner of High Road and Station Road, was burnt down by rioters protesting against the rejection of the Reform Bill in 1831, only five years after it had been built. At that time it employed about two hundred people. Twenty years later it employed 580 out of the town's total population of 3016. Now somewhat altered and dilapidated, it may be seen behind the modern shop-fronts and is the starting point for both the Beeston Old Village Trail and the South Beeston Industrial Trail. The latter also takes in the old Humber factory, where bicycles, motorcycles and cars were made until 1908,

Bennerley viaduct.

Boots' factory and offices, whose architecture ranges from 1928 to the present, and Shipstone's Maltings, built in the 1880s. Beeston's industry was assisted by being close to the railway and canal, and the trail passes the Midland Railway station of 1847, in a cottage style with bargeboards and latticed iron window frames, and the lock cottages built in 1796 for employees of the Beeston Canal.

Bennerley viaduct, Awsworth, Nottingham (OS 129: SK 472438).

The Great Northern Railway, in building a line from Friargate station, Derby, to Victoria station, Nottingham, found that between Ilkeston and Awsworth it had to cross the Erewash Canal, the river Erewash and the Nottingham Canal. In 1876-7, therefore, it built a 484 yard (443 metre) viaduct with sixteen spans, on piers 56 feet (17 metres) high. It is unusual in that it is one of only two in England made with wrought-iron lattice girders. The line is now disused, but the viaduct is still an impressive sight.

Bestwood winding house.

Bestwood winding house, Bestwood (OS 129: SK 556475).

The Bestwood Coal and Iron Company opened the colliery here in 1874, though iron smelting ceased in the 1920s and the colliery closed in 1967. The winding engine house, however, is a listed building and still stands, together with the headstocks. It is unique in that its steam-driven vertical winding engine remains intact. The area south of the winding house, which was the spoil heap, has now been landscaped into the Bestwood Country Park (page 47), which is the best place from which to view it.

Brinsley headstocks, Brinsley (OS 129: SK 467487).

Brinsley Colliery needed a second shaft by 1872 and it was sunk to a depth of 780 feet (238 metres). These tandem headstocks were put up to raise and lower the miners up and down the pit. Production ceased here in 1930 but it was kept open until 1970 for access to neighbouring collieries. All the buildings were demolished, the railway tracks taken up and

the site landscaped for a picnic area. The headstocks were re-erected here in their original position and are the centrepiece for a network of D. H. Lawrence trails.

Calverton framework knitters' cottages, Windles Square, Calverton, Nottingham (OS 129: SK 621491).

Calverton was the birthplace of William Lee, inventor of framework knitting (see page 111), and this became an important industry for the county. The cottages in Windles Square were built in 1834 around three sides of a rectangle, though one side has since been demolished. They are marked out by the large ground-floor windows, front and back, to give maximum light to the workers. This is typical of the locality, although elsewhere the large windows would be in an upper storey.

Further examples may be seen in Main Street, among them number 5, an eighteenth-century cottage, numbers 221-5, dated 1857, and on the opposite side of the road a work-shop built late in the eighteenth century and extended in the 1840s. Also in Main Street is the Calverton Folk Museum, open only by appointment (telephone: 0602 652836), which houses many items concerned with the hosiery trade as well as period furnishings.

Carlton Mill, Church Lane, Carlton in Lindrick, Worksop (OS 120: SK 588839).

The watermill is older than its nineteenth-century facelift would suggest and is most attractively situated by Carlton Lake. Its cast-iron undershot waterwheel is still in place, but when the flow of water was insufficient it was driven by steam power, hence the large chimney. It is now a museum, open by appointment only (telephone: 0909 730214). The mill machinery can be seen along with related exhibits, rural tools and collections of shells and butterflies.

Castle Mill, Linby (OS 120: SK 545510).

The river Leen was a hive of activity in the late eighteenth century, supplying power to no fewer than six cotton mills, owned by George Robinson and his sons. Most were strictly functional but, perhaps to keep up with the Byrons at nearby Newstead, this three-storey mill, formerly known simply as Upper Mill, has castellated towers at each corner of the façade. The pointed Gothic windows which completed the design were removed when it was converted into housing. Because of the problems with the water supply — the fifth Lord Byron played havoc with the river by damming it for the lake at Newstead — the Robinsons bought a Boulton & Watt steam engine in 1786 and became the first to apply steam power to a cotton mill. This was probably installed in Old Mill (SK 548502), now incorporated into Grange Farm, Papplewick. The other surviving Robinson mill is Forge Mill, Bestwood (SK 547471), a three-storey stone building of 1787.

Fiskerton Mill, Fiskerton, Southwell (OS 120: SK 742517).

The mill stands on the river Greet as it flows into the Trent and there has probably been one on this site since the twelfth century, when it was owned by the monks of Thurgarton Priory. The present building dates from about 1760 and was a lace-thread fac-

tory before being converted into a corn mill in 1837. An extensive fire in 1851, in which five people died, necessitated a thorough rebuild, though the older, smaller bricks are still evident at the sides and rear. It is four storeys high with seven bays and a pantiled roof.

Greens Mill, Windmill Lane, Sneinton, Nottingham. See page 89.

Kings Mill viaduct, Mansfield (OS 120: SK 520598).

The Mansfield & Pinxton Railway was opened in 1819 to carry stone to Pinxton Wharf on the Cromford Canal and coal back to Portland Wharf, Mansfield. This was before the invention of steam locomotives and the wagons were pulled by bullocks, and later by horses. This viaduct of five arches was built of local stone and displays a datestone 'M & P 1817'. It was taken over by the Midland Railway in 1848.

Littleborough Toll Cottage, Littleborough (OS 121: SK 815831).

The road from Littleborough ferry to Sturton-le-Steeple, although part of the Roman road known as Till Bridge Lane, between Lincoln to Doncaster, was in a poor condition until 1824 when an Act of Parliament was passed to enable it to be repaired by the levy of a toll at the turnpike. This isolated little hexagonal house was built of brick for the gatekeeper in 1825.

Longbottoms Mill, Great North Road, Tuxford (OS 120: SK 733717). Telephone: 0777 870413.

This is a four-storeyed nineteenth-century windmill, built of brick and tarred, with its machinery almost intact. Long out of use, it has now been restored with a new cap, fantail and sails and is open to the public at certain times.

Morleys' hosiery factory, Mansfield Road, Daybrook, Nottingham (OS 129: SK 580447).

I. & R. Morley started their lace and hosiery business at Sneinton in 1790, but this factory was built some seventy years later, two storeys high with eight bays and a large central clock. A three-storey extension was added to the

Framework knitters' cottages at Calverton, built in 1857, and (right) North Leverton windmill.

north in 1885 in a far more elaborate style with ornate brickwork, especially in the gable, and a more restrained four-storey extension was built to the east in 1901. The company closed its operations on this site in 1963.

North Leverton windmill, Mill Lane, North Leverton, Retford DN22 0AB (OS 120: SK 776821). Telephone: 0427 880662.
Open daily in the afternoon, except Tuesdays.
The windmill was built by a consortium of local farmers in 1813 and has been in use ever since. It was originally lower so that the cloth sails could be easily fitted from the ground, but in 1884 it was raised and given four patent sails. It is three storeys high, built of brick, tar-coated, and has an ogee cap and fantail. The machinery is in full working order and visitors may see it in action and buy some of the wholemeal flour. There is also a small exhibition about mills and milling.

Nottingham's industrial heritage
Nottingham is well served by museums, with the Industrial Museum, Canal Museum and Story of Nottingham Lace in particular

(pages 88-92), but a walk around the city will supplement an understanding of it as a commercial centre (see map on page 27).

The Nottingham Canal was built between 1792 and 1796 to compete with the Erewash Canal and follows much the same course from Eastwood, but just inside the county boundary, until turning sharply east near Trowell. It was 14³/4 miles (24 km) long, of which only half is left, and needed twenty locks to raise it 130 feet (40 metres) from the level of the Trent up to the Cromford Canal at Langley Mill, Derbyshire. Castle Lock, to the west of Wilford Street, is one of three which survive, and a good starting point for an industrial trail. The cast-iron boundary post on the south bank of the canal is unconnected with it but marked the limits of the old borough of Nottingham and the parish of Standard Hill. It bears the names of the overseers of the poor in 1869. Pass under the bridge, with its decorative steel panels, built in the 1900s, and on the left will be seen the British Waterways

Board's large brick warehouse of the same period. Further along is the Canal Museum (page 88), with its own basin under an arch in the building for easier loading and unloading, and its two Victorian hand cranes. Leaving the canal at the Carrington Street bridge, turn right for the Midland Station. The first station on this site was built in 1848, but this was felt to be insufficiently grand compared with the Great Central's Victoria Station, opened in 1900. The same architect, A. E. Lambert, was asked by the Midland Railway to design a new station for them, which was finished in 1904. It is of red terracotta and sandstone with a large central turret and conspicuous clock. The entrance and exit arches catch the eye, especially with their Art Nouveau wrought ironwork. The interior has escaped the worst excesses of British Rail's modernisation programme. To the right of the station is Queens Road, and at the far end is the Hicking Pentecost building of 1873, originally a tenement factory rented out to a variety

A cast-iron boundary marker by the canal in Nottingham and (right) Broadway, Nottingham.

of small lace manufacturers. Opposite this, on the other side of London Road, beyond the canal, is the Eastcroft Depot, a Victorian corporation depot with fanciful tower and spirelet. Turning left towards the city, notice on the right London Road Station. The Birkin family had an interest in the Great Northern Railway and it was their chosen architect, the Nottingham-born T. C. Hine, whose plans were commissioned in 1857. It is of two storeys, brick with a central gable and arched porch in his favoured mixture of Jacobean and Italian Renaissance style. Station Street bridge, over which it is approached, is a roving bridge, by which a horse towing a barge could cross from one bank of the canal to the other without needing to be unhitched.

From London Road carry on northwards up Bellar Gate and turn left along Hollowstone to St Mary's church (page 68), at the top of Stoney Street, to reach the area known as the Lace Market. On the left-hand side of Stoney Street is Broadway, laid out in 1855 by T. C. Hine for the lace manufacturer Richard Birkin. Their initials, together with those of the builders, Garland and Holland, appear over the main archway. The four-storey buildings run on either side of the road, which has a double curve halfway along to allow a more impressive façade. Opposite, in Plumptre Place is the Mills Building of 1906 with Art Nouveau wrought ironwork. Further along Stoney Street is the five-storey Barker Gate House of 1897, by the other major Victorian Nottingham architect, Watson Fothergill, in a more Arts and Crafts style. On the corner of Stoney Street and Warser Gate is the Adams & Page warehouse, one of Hine's most ambitious designs. Built in 1855 it has an E-shape ground plan with an imposing flight of steps to the entrance, four storeys high, again in the 'Anglo-Italian' style with much stone dressing on the façade. Adams & Page were comparatively enlightened employers, providing for their workers a tea room, classroom, library and chapel, whose more Gothic windows may be seen at pavement level. At the time it was considered far too grand for its purpose, but its architect maintained that, on the contrary, it merely showed how drab and unimaginative the civic buildings were. An

extension was needed only ten years later and the Warser Gate frontage is of this date. Note in particular the tympanum over the doorway depicting Britannia flanked by a merchant and a blacksmith, with ships, factories and a railway. Turn left into St Mary's Gate and right into Pilcher Gate. Here are two more warehouses: number 16, on the corner of Halifax Place, by Hine (*c.*1856) and, opposite, number 33, Milbie House, by Fothergill, one of his more restrained, symmetrical designs. To return to the starting point, turn left into Fletcher Gate and right into Middle Pavement, which leads into Maid Marian Way. Wilford Street is at the bottom of the hill.

Ollerton Watermill, Ollerton (OS 120: SK 653673).

There has been a watermill on this site since Norman times, but the present one dates from the early eighteenth century. It is built in brick and roofed with pantiles. The machinery is all in working order and the iron waterwheel, driven by the river Maun, is dated 1862. Visits may be made, preferably by appointment.

Papplewick Pumping Station, off Longdale Lane, Ravenshead, Nottingham NG15 9AJ (OS 120: SK 584522). Telephone: 0602 632938.
Open Sunday afternoons 31st March to 27th October; in steam Bank Holiday and certain other weekends.

The provision of water to Nottingham, with its rapidly increasing population, in the nineteenth century was a major problem and required no less than three pumping stations to be built in the space of 27 years. Papplewick was the last of these, designed by Marriot Ogle Tarbotton, engineer to the Corporation of Nottingham, which had just taken charge of the privately owned waterworks company that previously supplied the city's needs. It was at his urgent recommendation that it was built in 1882-4. Housing two beam engines by James Watt & Company and fired by six Lancashire boilers, it was capable of pumping 3 million gallons (13.6 million litres) of water a day. The building is of red brick, with comparatively modest ornament, and is quite

Papplewick Pumping Station.

attractive, seen from across the 1,250,000 gallon (5.7 million litre) cooling pond. Inside, not only are the engines breathtaking, but the cast-iron columns and galleries are highly decorated with four storks or cranes as capitals. Stained glass completes the atmosphere in this temple to industry.

The second pumping station is at Bestwood (SK 579482), built by Thomas Hawksley in 1873 in an Italian Gothic style, with a sort of campanile to disguise the chimney. The engines have been removed. The first, at Basford, was built in 1857 but demolished in 1970, when one of its engines was transferred to the Nottingham Industrial Museum (page 91). Also on the Papplewick site are a working steam winding engine from a local colliery and a miniature steam railway that carries passengers.

Pickford's Depository, Worksop (OS 120: SK 585793).

The Chesterfield Canal was the first to be built in Nottinghamshire, stretching from Chesterfield in Derbyshire to West Stockwith on the Trent, 46 miles (74 km) in all, with 65 locks and two tunnels. The route was surveyed by the foremost canal engineer of the time, James Brindley, but most of the work, which started in 1771, was carried out under the supervision of his deputy, John Varley, and took six years. It was taken over by the Sheffield & Lincoln Junction Railway in 1846 and efficiently run until 1863, when the company decided to let the operation run down. The collapse of the Norwood Tunnel in 1908 cut off the Chesterfield end of the canal and

hastened the decline.

In the early nineteenth century, when the depository was built, the canal was in its heyday. It is a three-storey building of yellow brick, with small windows but large double doors on the ground and first floors. Half of it spans the canal and there are trap-doors in the stone archway to load and unload the 'cuckoos', as the narrow-boats peculiar to this canal were called.

Shipley Lock aqueduct, Eastwood, Nottingham (OS 129: SK 462455).

The Erewash Canal was built in 1777-9 to provide easy transport from the coalfields. It is nearly 12 miles (19 km) long, running south from Langley Mill, Derbyshire, to join the Trent at Trent Lock. At Shipley Lock an aqueduct takes the canal across the Erewash river. This was achieved by building the canal first and diverting the river underneath it.

Stapleford framework knitters' cottages, Nottingham Road, Stapleford (OS 129: SK 495374).

Framework knitting was an important industry to Stapleford. Numbers 106-12 Nottingham Road are an early nineteenth-century terrace of three-storey brick houses. The large windows on the top storey immediately proclaim them to be the dwellings and workshops of framework knitters, who needed as much natural light as possible on their work. Numbers 118-22 and 119-21 are slightly later but still display the same characteristic. Broom Hill Terrace at Bramcote (SK 506379) is a similar row of cottages, dating from the 1830s.

Trent Valley power stations

There are thirteen power stations in the valley of the Trent and its tributaries, producing nearly one quarter of all the power generated in Britain, hence the nickname of 'Megawatt Valley'. Of these, five are in Nottinghamshire. It was the close proximity of coalfields and of sufficient water to cool the steam that made the Trent such a suitable site for the generation of electricity. Of the early power stations, Wilford (built in 1925) and the postwar Staythorpe A have now been demolished and Staythorpe B, commissioned in 1960, produces electricity only on demand. Since it is only comparatively small, it does not require the massive cooling towers, which are 374 feet (114 metres) high, with a maximum diameter of 305 feet (93 metres), that are such a distinguishing feature of the others. High Marnham, the first 1000 megawatt power station, began production in 1959 and was followed by three more of 2000 megawatts in quick succession: Ratcliffe on Soar (1967), West Burton (1968) and Cottam (1969). With the effects of privatisation, nuclear power and the contraction of the coal industry, it is unlikely that any more of this nature will be built in the county in the future.

Wilford Bridge tollhouse, Nottingham (OS 129: SK 569383).

Wilford Bridge was built in 1870, as an alternative to the narrow brick and stone Trent Bridge. It was designed by E. W. Hughes, with cast ironwork by Handyside of Derby, but suffered badly from corrosion and was taken down in 1982. The approaches remain, with a modern footbridge over the river. The brick tollhouse was built in a Gothic style to collect the charges, under the 1862 Wilford Bridge Act, that are displayed above the door. It can never have been very profitable since in 1871 a new Trent Bridge was erected by the Corporation Engineer, M. Ogle Tarbotton (see also Papplewick Pumping Station, page 101), with cast ironwork also by Handyside.

Pickford's Depository, Worksop.

9
Other places to visit

Abbeydale Farm Centre, Longdale Lane, Ravenshead, Nottingham NG15 9AH. Telephone: 0623 792270.
Open daily.

Rare breeds of farm animals are the focus of attention here, with Gloucester Old Spot, Tamworth and Saddleback pigs, Dexter and Highland cattle and several types of goat, including Angora and Anglo-Nubian. There are a variety of ducks and poultry and also small animals, such as rabbits, for the children to make a fuss of.

The Bramley Apple Display, Merryweather Garden Centre, Halam Road, Southwell NG25 0AH. Telephone: 0636 813204.
Open daily. Teashop.

The first Bramley apple tree grew from the chance planting of a seed around the year

The Lace Centre, Severns, seen from the walls of Nottingham Castle.

1805. It acquired its name from a later owner, Matthew Bramley. In 1856 Henry Merryweather, a nurseryman, took grafts from the tree and its fame spread from then on. This display tells its history and reconstructs a corner of Henry Merryweather's office with contemporary pictures, books and nursery catalogues.

Butterflies Pleasure Park, The White Post, Farnsfield, Newark NG22 8HX. Telephone: 0623 882773.
Open daily. Café.

The Tropical House is the main attraction, with exotic plants, birds and many species of butterflies. The native butterflies are not neglected, however, and a wild-flower meadow provides suitable habitat for, amongst others, holly blues, brimstones, red admirals and peacocks. There are also an adventure playground, a grass maze, crazy golf and mini-golf, and a pets' corner.

Dukeries Adventure Park and Picnic Area, Welbeck, Worksop S80 3LT. Telephone: 0909 476506.
Open daily Easter to September.

This supervised play area provides a number of activities including towers and a rock face to climb, an aerial runway, rope bridges, slides, tube slide, ball pool and bouncy castle.

The Lace Centre, Severns, Castle Road, Nottingham NG1 6AA. Telephone: 0602 413539.
Open daily except Christmas Day.

This fifteenth-century timber-framed house with tiled roof was moved to its present position from Middle Pavement in the late 1960s and was restored at that time to something like its original state. The first-floor windows were copied from a contemporary house in Exeter. It has a crown-post roof structure, unusual for the East Midlands, and seems to have been part of a larger building. Inside is the Lace Centre, an exhibition selling Nottingham lace, which also has some displays on the history of lacemaking.

Nottingham Brass Rubbing Centre, St Mary the Virgin, High Pavement, Nottingham NG1 1HF. Telephone: 0602 582105.
Open Tuesday to Saturday, and also Sundays in summer.

There are a number of facsimile brasses available for rubbing, including the one to Richard Willoughby (died 1471) and his wife from Wollaton church (page 75).

The Nottingham Story, City Information Centre, 1-4 Smithy Row, Nottingham NG1 2BY. Telephone: 0602 483500, extension 4430.
Open daily except Sunday.

An audio-visual display, lasting 25 minutes, presents a portrait of Nottingham, its history and attractions (available on request in foreign languages).

Playworld, Floralands Garden Centre, Catfoot Lane, Lambley, Nottingham NG4 4QL. Telephone: 0602 670487.
Open daily from April to August, also weekends and school holidays in September and October. Coffee shop.

Playworld is a children's playpark, with a wide variety of activities. It has an assault course, bouncy castle, sandpit, slides and helter-skelter, amongst other attractions, and a real fire-engine for youngsters to play on.

Reg Taylor's Swan Sanctuary, Hill Farm Nurseries, Normanton, Southwell NG25 0PR. Telephone: 0636 813184.
Open daily. Tearooms.

Four lakes have been excavated on a 9 acre (3.5 hectare) site, the spoil cleverly contoured and several thousand trees planted to form a home for injured swans and other wildfowl. For some it is a temporary refuge until they recover, but more severely damaged birds stay permanently. With the establishment of indigenous wild flowers and careful management, the area has quickly developed into a nature reserve. Visitors are encouraged to feed the swans and good access and pathways are available for the disabled.

Sherwood Forest Amusement Park, Sherwood Country Park, Edwinstowe, Mansfield NG21 9QA. Telephone: 0623 823536.
Open weekends in March, daily over Easter and from May to September, weekends in October.

This is a permanent funfair, with many of the traditional attractions, including dodgems, a ghost train, slides and roundabouts.

Sherwood Forest Farm Park, Lamb Pens Farm, Edwinstowe, Mansfield NG21 9HL. Telephone: 0623 823558.
Open daily April to mid October. Tearooms.

The main attractions here are the thirty different rare and interesting breeds of farm animals. There are Soay, Hebridean and Herdwick sheep, Middle White and Tamworth pigs, Gloucester, Highland and Dexter cattle, amongst others, as well as poultry, black swans, geese and 25 types of waterfowl. Wild animals include fallow deer, water buffalo and chipmunks, and a large aviary houses a variety of colourful birds. For children there are a pets' corner and play area, and for adults more than an acre of beautiful gardens and a tea room specialising in home-made cakes.

Sundown Kiddies Adventureland and Pets Garden, Treswell Road, Rampton, Retford DN22 0HX. Telephone: 0777 248274.
Open daily except Christmas Day and Boxing Day. Tearooms.

This theme park caters especially for children under ten, providing safe scenarios for them to act out their favourite stories, be it in the Pirate Ship, Noah's Ark, Western Street, Tudor Village or Magic Castle. There are nursery-rhyme tableaux, a miniature farm with animals and birds and a playground to keep younger children amused.

The Tales of Robin Hood, 30/38 Maid Marian Way, Nottingham NG1 6GF. Telephone: 0602 483284.
Open daily except Christmas Eve, Christmas Day and Boxing Day. Restaurant.

Here is proof, if any more be needed, of the

enduring appeal of Robin Hood. The heart of the visit is a chair ride following his adventures from imprisonment by the Sheriff to feasting in Sherwood Forest. Elements of five of the six earliest medieval tales are woven into the sequence and the settings, from the fletcher's workshop to the watermill, are as historically accurate as possible. Even the atmosphere changes as the journey progresses, such as the smoke of the smithy and the chill of the hermit's cave. After the trip one can study the history of the legend, medieval weaponry and a little about Nottingham and Sherwood Forest. A fifteen-minute audiovisual presentation imaginatively depicts a 1930s detective searching for clues to the real Robin Hood. There is plenty of Robin Hood memorabilia, especially books, games and film posters. Archery practice is an optional extra.

Tumble Town, 107B High Street, Arnold, Nottingham NG5 7DS. Telephone: 0602 671161.
Open daily. Café.
This is an indoor play area designed for children up to eight years old, offering safe and supervised activities including climbing frames, helter-skelters, bouncing castle, ball pools and hanging men.

Wetlands Waterfowl Reserve and Exotic Bird Park, Lound Low Road, Sutton cum Lound, Retford DN22 8SB. Telephone: 0777 818099.
Open daily except Christmas Day. Café.
This is a park of 32 acres (13 hectares) comprising mixed woodland, grassland and lakes, which were formerly sandpits, now flooded. It is a pleasant setting for a wide variety of swans, geese, ducks and flamingos from all parts of the world. Although the waterfowl are the main attraction, there are also peacocks, parrots and other exotic birds and a number of farmyard birds and animals, including some rare breeds.

White Post Modern Farm Centre, White Post Farm, Farnsfield, Newark NG22 8HL.

Telephone: 0623 882977.
Open daily. Tearooms.
The Farm Centre is part of a working farm and sets out not only to entertain but also to explain everything around the farm. There are plenty of tame animals, from rabbits to llamas, to stroke, as well as newly hatched chicks to see in the incubator room and piglets in the outdoor breeding unit. Children are encouraged to gain first-hand experience of crops, as well as animals, by learning from games and display boards. Other features are the butterflies, spiders, fish and turtles and you can handle the snakes if you feel so inclined!

Wild Flower Farm Visitors Centre, Coach Gap Lane, Langar, Nottingham NG13 9HP. Telephone: 0949 60592.
Open from Easter to September, Fridays to Sundays and Bank Holiday Mondays.
As part of a commercial venture selling wild-flower plants, seeds, trees and shrubs, visitors are encouraged to explore the wildflower meadows, where well over a hundred varieties may be seen. The flowers are not only beautiful in their own right but also attract numerous butterflies, insects, birds and small mammals. Refreshments are available.

The World of Robin Hood, Haughton, Retford DN22 8DZ. Telephone: 0623 860210.
Open daily in summer and on weekends, school and public holidays in winter.
The sets used for the film *Robin Hood — Prince of Thieves* have been brought together to form the basis for this trip back to the time of Richard I. By the use of holograms and other modern technology, medieval characters give a commentary as the tour progresses from a Crusader castle, through an open-air medieval village street with its market, to Sherwood Forest and on to Nottingham Castle. Visitors are given an opportunity to handle medieval weapons — longbow and crossbow as well as swords and axes — and there are siege engines on display. Some of Robin Hood's adventures are re-enacted as a special event on certain days.

10
Famous people

Bendigo (William Thompson, 1811-80)

William and his two brothers were born as triplets to a slum family with eighteen children already. They were soon nicknamed Shadrach, Meshach and Abednego, hence his name. Although he gained fame as a barefisted prizefighter, he was known locally not only for his physical strength but also as a batsman and angler. It is recorded that he threw a cricket ball 115 yards (105 metres) and for a bet hurled a brick 75 yards (68.5 metres), with his left hand, over the river Trent. At the age of 28 he was proclaimed Champion Boxer of England. Three of his most famous fights were with another well-known Nottinghamshire prizefighter, Ben Caunt of Hucknall. Their final contest went 93 rounds and lasted two hours ten minutes, with the decision given in favour of Bendigo. At the age of 39 he retired unbeaten, the first recorded southpaw. He took to the bottle and served 28 terms in jail for being drunk and disorderly.

After attending a revivalist meeting he repented of his ways and became famous as a preacher of abstinence. He settled in Beeston, joining the Ebenezer Lodge of Good Templars. His meetings were so popular and well-attended that a well-known hymn was amended to:

Praise God from whom all blessings flow,
Praise Him for Brother Bendigo...

On 23rd August 1880 he died, aged 69, after falling downstairs. His funeral cortège was followed by thousands to his final resting place in Bath Street Cemetery, Nottingham.

Two other well-known boxers were bred in the county. **Jem Mace** (1831-1911) was considered one of the greatest figures in the age of the pugilists. Born in Beeston of gypsy parentage, he was the last important figure in the British prize ring before the introduction of gloved fighting.

John Shaw (died 1815) came from Wollaton. He joined the Lifeguards in 1807 and gained national recognition although he fought only two prize fights. He was badly injured at the battle of Waterloo and died a few days later.

Jesse Boot (1850-1931)

Jesse Boot began his working life in his mother's herbalist shop. His father, a farm labourer, had died when Jesse was ten and his widow had continued running the shop, which had been started as a sideline at 6 Goosegate, Nottingham. During this time Jesse studied to improve his knowledge of drugs and gradually took over the business, forming in 1888 the Boots Pure Drug Company. The name was chosen because, in the price war which he started locally, he had been accused of selling adulterated goods. His success came because he realised the potential of bulk buying, thus keeping prices to a minimum. His company prospered, so that by 1896 the firm owned a chain of sixty shops. He expanded the range of goods sold in the shops, apparently at the suggestion of his wife, Florence, to include stationery, books, jewellery, silverware and art. He sold the company to an American concern in 1920 but his son bought it back again during the depression in 1933.

Jesse was knighted in 1903, created a baronet in 1917, mainly for his philanthropy to the city, and raised to the peerage in 1929, two years before his death. The foundations for the present university campus were laid when he acquired the Highfields site in 1920 and gave £150,000 towards the building and an endowment fund; it is estimated that in all he donated about £2 million to the city.

Jesse Boot spent the last thirty years of his life crippled with rheumatoid arthritis, eventually unable to do anything for himself. He was so ill that he could not attend the opening of the University Buildings by King George V and Queen Mary. There is a bronze bust of him at the entrance gates to the park on University Boulevard. He died in Jersey in 1931.

William Booth (1829-1912)

The founder of the Salvation Army was born on l0th April 1829 at 12 Notintone Place, a small terraced house in Sneinton, Nottingham, where his parents lived until 1831. They then moved to a smallholding in Bleasby, returning to West Street in Nottingham from 1835 to 1843. He went to school at Biddulph's Academy, a commercial day school run by the educationalist and Methodist preacher Sampson Biddulph in the Sion Chapel in Halifax Place (now the Lace Market Theatre). At thirteen he had to leave, as his father was made bankrupt, and he was apprenticed to Francis Eames of Belward Street, a pawnbroker. Shortly after, because of her husband's death, his mother was forced to move to Goosegate, Nottingham, where she kept a shop selling toys and tape, needles and cotton. William Booth's sisters continued this business at number 5 Hockley for many years. It was here that he saw the appalling living conditions of so many people in the nineteenth century and was inspired to try to relieve such hardship in his later work.

His conversion came in 1844 at the Wesley Chapel, Broad Street (now the Co-operative Education Centre). A year later he had a call to preach the gospel and gave his first sermon in a house in Kid Street; and so at the age of seventeen William Booth became a Methodist preacher. Much of his time was spent preaching on street corners in the Hockley and Stoney Street areas of Nottingham. In one famous incident, he upset the congregation of the Wesley Chapel by allowing his converts to burst through the main entrance and fill the best seats. His 'gang of slummers' was soon required to use the back entrance in Heathcoat Street and had to sit on obscure wooden benches behind the pulpit. Not surprisingly he was a supporter of the fiery Irish Chartist, Feargus O'Connor, Nottingham's Member of Parliament at the time.

At the age of twenty, he left Nottingham for London and became a Methodist minister. Finding church structures too much of a constraint, he resigned and in 1865 started the Christian Missions, which subsequently became the Salvation Army in 1878. Initially William Booth opposed the use of military titles, now so much part of the movement, but eventually he agreed to their use. In the early years the Salvation Army workers were subjected to physical violence and persecution because of the areas in which they worked. However, despite this, by the 1880s the movement had spread to the United States, South America, Australia, France, India and South Africa. It continues to this day as a worldwide Christian organisation prepared to venture to many dangerous but needy places to bring messages of hope and practical social care.

In 1905 William Booth was made a freeman of the City of Nottingham, where his name is still honoured. Many sites associated with him are still standing in the city and his birthplace is now a museum and part of the William Booth Memorial Complex (open by appointment, telephone: 0602 503927).

Samuel Butler (1835-1902)

The grandson and namesake of the educationalist Dr Samuel Butler was born at the Rectory in Langar-cum-Barnstone. From his later writings it is evident that he had an unhappy childhood, being subjected to corporal punishment and receiving little affection. He was educated at Shrewsbury and St John's College, Cambridge, where he studied mathematics and classics. In response to pressure from his father, he left England in 1859 and travelled to New Zealand. There he became a successful sheep farmer and started to write. Five years later, selling the farm, he returned to London and settled in chambers off Fleet Street. Although he had written controversial articles while in New Zealand, his plan on his return was to take up a career as an artist. During the next six years he produced a number of paintings. The novel *Erewhon*, a fantasy partly based on his life in New Zealand, was published in 1872. In it he described a world whose values had been turned upside down. A second book, *The Fair Haven*, followed in 1873. The same year he started his best-known work, *The Way of All Flesh*. It is largely autobiographical but was not published until after his death. More books flowed from his pen as he turned his attention to Darwin's *Origin of Species* and during the next ten years he attacked the theories in

The statue of William Booth in front of his birthplace in Sneinton and (right) the bust of Lord Byron by the main entrance of the Castle Museum in Nottingham.

several works.

Butler continued his unorthodox scholarship in publishing his own theory that the *Odyssey* was written by a woman. His largest work was a two-volume edition of his grandfather's life and letters, and, coming full circle, his final book was *Erewhon Revisited*. He died in St John's Wood, London, in June 1902.

Lord Byron (George Gordon Byron, 1788-1824)

The renowned poet was the son of Captain 'Mad Jack' Byron and Catherine Gordon of Gight, a Scottish heiress. She was abandoned by her husband before the birth of her son, in London, on 22nd January 1788. Byron was brought up in Aberdeen in relative poverty, since his father had squandered his mother's fortune before his premature death in 1791.

He inherited the title as sixth Lord Byron, unexpectedly, at the age of ten, but the state of Newstead Abbey was such that he spent much of his time elsewhere in Nottinghamshire. At various times he lodged at 76 St James Street, Nottingham, at Burgage Manor, Southwell, and in the Clinton Arms Hotel and in chambers at Newark. He did live at Newstead intermittently from 1809 to 1814.

Byron was educated at Harrow and Cambridge but never forgot the squalor and poverty he had seen in his childhood. In his maiden speech in the House of Lords he unsuccessfully espoused the cause of the framework knitters.

The travels he undertook around the Mediterranean and the Middle East provided much material for his most popular works, especially *Childe Harold's Pilgrimage*. Following its publication, he was lionised by London society. After a long courtship he married Annabella Milbanke in 1815 but separated from her within a year. He became notorious for his excesses and, following several well-known love affairs including a very public one with Lady Caroline Lamb, who would not leave him alone, and rumours of an illicit relationship with his half-sister Augusta Leigh, he was ostracised by society. He went into self-imposed exile, never to return, although he continued to write and his fame grew. His last, unfinished work, *Don Juan*, was started in 1822.

On 19th April 1824 he died at Missolonghi in Greece, of a fever, at the age of 36. His body was brought back to England and lay in state at the Blackamoor's Head in Pelham Street, Nottingham, having been refused burial in Westminster Abbey. Immense crowds, many of them stockingers, followed his cortège. He was buried in the family vault in Hucknall church.

Thomas Cranmer (1489-1556)

Henry VIII's most influential archbishop was brought up in Aslockton and attended a local grammar school, possibly at Southwell. He worshipped in nearby Whatton church, leaving Nottinghamshire at the age of fourteen for Cambridge. After an obscure career as a theologian and archdeacon, he was selected by Henry VIII in 1533 and was the last Archbishop of Canterbury appointed both by Rome and with the approval of the King. His elevation was probably due to his suggestion that the 'King's Great Matter' (his divorce from Catherine of Aragon) should be referred to the universities for resolution. One of his first acts, following his consecration, was to pronounce the marriage null and void, After Anne Boleyn's death he pronounced that marriage also invalid and granted Henry a divorce from Anne of Cleves. His time in office lasted for a remarkable 23 years in a period when the King's displeasure could mean an untimely end. In 1534 the anti-papal legislation became statutory and the practice of the Crown nominating bishops was brought into effect. However, much of the political and organisational break with Rome was directed by the King and Thomas Cromwell.

Cranmer left his mark on the Church of England and it was under his influence that the Thirty-nine Articles were written (42 in his time). He drafted the Litany, Morning and Evening Prayer and translated and composed the Collects.

He never wavered in his loyalty to the King and, although he served through Edward VI's reign, did not have as close a relationship with him. He was convicted of treason against Queen Mary I in an ecclesiastical court, found guilty of heresy and burnt at the stake at Oxford on 21st March 1556.

Nottinghamshire also provided two other Archbishops of Canterbury. **Thomas Secker** (Archbishop 1758-68) came from Sibthorpe and, although he did not publish any works, was considered in his day to be a competent scholar, an eminent Hebraist. He had qualified as a doctor of medicine in Leiden. **Charles Manners Sutton** (Archbishop 1805-28), from Kelham, was the grandson of the third Duke of Rutland and a most conscientious Primate, financially very astute. He was not a great scholar but he did publish a small botanical work on an obscure plant.

Robin Hood

All our knowledge of Robin Hood comes from literature. There is no accurate historical record, although there is evidence that someone of that name may have existed. The first time the legend of Robin Hood appears is in about 1377 in William Langland's *Piers the Plowman*. The stories, mentioned in passing, are noted with some disparagement. The earliest ballads dealing directly with Robin Hood were written down in the late fifteenth century; the most famous, *The Lyttell Geste of Robyn Hode*, was printed about 1500 and contains 456 verses. This is almost certainly based on a number of stories put together possibly as much as a hundred years earlier. Popular tales often place Robin as a contemporary of King Richard I; this is now thought unlikely and, if he did exist, using the internal evidence of the early ballads, his dates seem more likely to be within the thirteenth century, most probably in the reign of Henry III (1216-72).

Most modern versions associate Robin with Sherwood Forest and the Sheriff of Nottingham, whereas the scraps of evidence for a historical character place him in the Barnsdale area of Yorkshire. This is borne out by the mention of Yorkshire place-names in the *Geste*. However, part of the action in *Robin Hood and the Potter* takes place in Nottingham. Some experts feel that the association with the Sheriff of Nottingham is a merging of two separate traditions. On the other hand, it does seem likely that the area of operation of a band of outlaws of that period would be wide and Barnsdale is only 30 miles (48 km) from Sherwood Forest.

Unfortunately, many of the characters now associated with Robin are later additions. The office of Sheriff of Nottingham was not created until 1449. There were, however, Sheriffs of Nottinghamshire and Derbyshire, some of whom were not very popular, and at certain times they would have had to travel through Sherwood Forest to York to present accounts of their stewardship to the King's officers. Little John does occur in the *Geste* and in the other ballads. Maid Marion first appears much later, in the sixteenth century, although French ballads mention her name in other contexts. Friar Tuck is likewise a later addition, but there may have been a Sussex outlaw with a similar name in the early fifteenth century.

Despite this confusing picture, Robin Hood and his exploits still flourish in Sherwood Forest and a walk through the woods can help the imagination to conjure up some of the exciting, if improbable, tales that have been told about the folk hero and his band of merry men.

David Herbert Lawrence (1885-1930)

Son of a miner from the Brinsley Pit and a former schoolteacher, Lawrence was born at 8a Victoria Street, Eastwood (now a museum, page 85). The family moved to various houses in the town during his childhood. He was educated first at Beauvale Boys School, Dovecote Road, Hill Top (still used as a local school), and was the first Eastwood boy to win a county scholarship to Nottingham High School, where he studied from 1898 to 1901. He was not an outstanding scholar and, having left school, worked first as a clerk in Nottingham and then as an uncertificated teacher in Eastwood. In 1906 he undertook a two-year training course at University College, Nottingham (now occupied by Nottingham Trent University). After graduation he moved to Croydon to teach. In 1912 he eloped with his former professor's wife, Frieda Weekley, and left England hurriedly. They married a few years later.

A Prelude, a Christmas story, his first published work, appeared in the *Weekly Guardian* in 1907. *Sons and Lovers* was published in 1913, with a strong autobiographical element, and some of his portrayals of personalities, and especially of his father, caused resentment locally. The book also provides many descriptions of the countryside of his childhood.

Lawrence moved back to England during the First World War but was unable to find a settled place to live, partly because of his wife's German origins and the scandal that still followed him. However, during this time he published *Women in Love* (1921) but again started his travels in 1922, visiting Australia and Mexico. In 1926 he was diagnosed as having tuberculosis and spent time in Italy and Austria trying, unsuccessfully, to find a cure. Whilst in Florence, he wrote his most controversial novel, *Lady Chatterley's Lover*, published in 1928, though the full text did not appear until 1960 and was the object of a significant court case. He died in Vence near Nice, France, of tuberculosis in 1930.

William Lee (1564-1610)

Very little is known about Lee and even his dates are calculated rather than documented. He is designated as a curate but there is no evidence that he took holy orders. It is believed that he gained an MA from Cambridge and it is likely that he may have helped out in the village church at Calverton.

Some of the suggested reasons why he invented the stocking frame are romantic but wrong. There is no information about his wife or sweetheart or the woman knitter that he was supposed to be trying to outdo.

What is known is that he perfected his frame by 1589, and attempted to gain a patent from Queen Elizabeth I to develop the machine, but this was refused. Eventually he went to Paris, where he attracted the attention of Henry of Navarre and the promise of support, but Henry was assassinated before any

The church at Babworth where Richard Clyfton was rector.

money was forthcoming. William Lee is thought to have died in Paris in 1610. His brother, James Lee, brought the stocking frame back to London, where the industry developed. It moved to the Midlands later in the century and has since settled in the area. It was William Lee's basic ideas which laid the foundation of the hosiery industry as we now know it.

Arthur Mee (1875-1943)

Born in Stapleford on 21st July 1875, Mee received his education at the village school, since renamed the Arthur Mee Centre. He first joined the *Nottingham Evening Post* at the age of fourteen but soon moved to the *Express*, which was more in keeping with his sympathies, as his father, who brought him up, was a militant nonconformist. Five years later he went to London, where he found his niche writing for the youth of the country. He edited the *Children's Newspaper*, the *Children's Encyclopedia*, the *Children's Shakespeare* and the *Children's Bible*. He is perhaps best remembered for his work on *The King's England*, a series of guidebooks surveying ten thousand towns and villages which ran to eighty volumes and is still a useful source of information.

The Pilgrim Fathers

When the *Mayflower* eventually sailed from Plymouth on 6th September 1620 it was the culmination of much religious activity, dissent and persecution going back over thirty years. The ship carried 102 passengers, many of whom came from the north Midlands, two of the more notable leaders being William Bradford and William Brewster from Nottinghamshire.

William Bradford (1589-1657) was younger than many of the Pilgrim Fathers. He was born of a prominent local family in 1589 at Austerfield, just over the border in Yorkshire. He had to withstand their opposition to his beliefs, at a time when disagreement with, and non-attendance at, the local parish church meant risking harsh penalties. However, he persisted in his beliefs and joined the separatist community at Scrooby. Richard Clyfton, deprived of his living as Rector of Babworth, became their pastor and gave him much support. It was through his influence that Bradford went to Holland and thence to America with the *Mayflower*.

It is from William Bradford's writings that much of the work of the Pilgrim Fathers is known. He became the second governor of the Plymouth Plantation, and his wise rule lasted from 1621 until his death in 1657.

William Brewster (1566-1644) is associated with the village of Scrooby, where he followed in his father's footsteps and was Master of Posts, responsible for the safe and speedy delivery of messages in the area from Tuxford to Doncaster. He was educated at Cambridge, where he first heard dissenting preachers, and spent some time in the service of Queen Elizabeth I as a junior diplomat and an assistant to the Secretary of State.

Brewster's religious sympathies crystallised when in 1606 he joined with the Brownist clergy and people of the area to found the first independent congregation of separatists in Scrooby, which met in his house. He was forced to flee to Holland, following a time of imprisonment in Boston, and set up a print shop in Leiden. From there he sent back pamphlets to England expounding the puritan and separatist causes. It was from Leiden that he joined the *Speedwell*, planning to travel with the *Mayflower* for the journey to the New World. The *Speedwell* proved to be unseaworthy, so those who could boarded the *Mayflower* for the voyage.

William Brewster died at the age of 78 in 1644, having been the main author of the Mayflower Compact, a new constitution which enabled the election of a governor for the colony, the first step towards democracy in the history of the English colonies.

The Regicides

The Midlands were the scene of some of the more significant battles during the Civil War. As elsewhere, many families were divided, some members supporting the Royalist cause, others that of Parliament. Although Nottinghamshire was on the whole Royalist, the people of Nottingham supported Parliament. There were five notable Parliamentarians in the area, all of whom were involved directly in the death sentence on King Charles I, executed on 30th January 1649.

Francis Hacker (1618-60) was born in East Bridgford though the family later moved to Colston Bassett. He was the only member of his family to support the Parliamentarians. His wife, Isabella, was a relative of Samuel Brunts, the founder of the Brunts Charity in Mansfield.

Hacker was described as a fine soldier and a militia commander who was especially active in Leicestershire. At one stage in the war he was captured and held for some time in Belvoir Castle.

His main claim to fame is as King Charles's warder. He was responsible for the King whilst he was held in London and was, according to his lights, compassionate to him. The warrant for the King's execution was addressed to him and to two others; they were required to ensure that the King was beheaded on 30th January. Hacker escorted the King to the place of execution and helped supervise the order.

During the Commonweath Hacker remained a staunch supporter of Oliver Cromwell, and he became a Member of Parliament for Leicester in Richard Cromwell's time. At the Restoration he was arrested, put on trial, condemned and executed on the gallows at Tyburn on 19th October 1660. He is buried in Cole Abbey, London.

Colonel John Hutchinson (1615-64) was one of the more unusual Parliamentarians, being described as reserved by nature, polite and fashionable of dress. He was closely connected to many of the Royalist families in the area, and his mother had been a Byron. His wife, Lucy, daughter of Sir Allen Apsley, Lieutenant of the Tower of London, had a brother who fought for the King. They, however, both espoused the Puritan cause. He was appointed Parliamentary Governor of Nottingham, defending the castle against attacks on several occasions. During the first attack, snipers used St Nicholas church tower to harass the castle, so Hutchinson razed the church to the ground when the siege was lifted. Despite this, on the whole he is reported to have treated his enemies well and to have behaved in an honourable fashion. He was one of the 59 signatories to the death warrant.

His distrust of Cromwell grew and, whilst he still had some influence, he persuaded Parliament, in 1651, to order the destruction of Nottingham Castle in order to thwart Cromwell's ambitions. In 1652 he returned to Owthorpe, his family home, where he rebuilt the house, which had been sacked several times by Royalist troops, giving hospitality to oppressed Royalist relatives. At the Restoration in 1660 he was a member of the convention which welcomed the return of Charles II. Later he was pardoned by the Act of Oblivion. In 1663 he was arrested for complicity in the Northern Plot, though this was never proved. After imprisonment in the Tower of London he was transferred to Sandown Castle in Kent, where in appalling conditions he caught a fever and died on 11th September 1664. His widow brought his body back to Owthorpe for burial.

Attenborough was the birthplace of **Henry Ireton** (1611-51), who is considered to have been one of the finest commanders on the Parliamentary side. The Ireton family house still stands near the parish church. Henry studied law at Trinity College, Oxford, but chose to become a military and political adviser to the Parliamentary army. An able soldier, he fought at Edgehill, Gainsborough, Naseby (where he was injured and captured but managed to escape) and at Bristol.

His wife, Bridget, was Oliver Cromwell's daughter and a close friendship developed between the two men. He was nicknamed 'the Scribe' because he was not only competent at drafting reports and legislation but also articulate and wordy.

At first he tried to save the King until he became aware that the King was not to be trusted. Then he enthusiastically accepted the appointment as one of the judges who tried the King and was a signatory to the death warrant.

He became Lord Deputy in Ireland, where he served under Cromwell, dying of swamp fever in Limerick in 1651. Following the Restoration, his body was exhumed from Westminster Abbey, hanged at Tyburn and then buried in a deep pit under the gallows.

Gilbert Millington (1584-1666) was probably born about 1584 and lived in Felley House near Annesley. Little of good report is known about him. He represented Nottingham in the Long Parliament but contributed little to it, being weak and unreliable. He gained his place through social position rather than by ability. Throughout the period there was antagonism between him and Colonel Hutchinson. Lucy Hutchinson reports that at sixty, following the death of his first wife, he married an alehouse wench of sixteen and that this caused much outrage to local puritan morals.

He was put on trial as a regicide but played on his deafness and age — he was by now 76. The death sentence was pronounced on him following the verdict of guilty but it was commuted to life imprisonment. He died in Jersey in 1666.

The Whalley family had lived in Screveton for generations. **Edward Whalley** (died 1675) was a wealthy woollen draper living in Kirketon Hall, and as soon as war broke out he joined the Parliamentarians. A cousin of Oliver Cromwell and related to the Hacker family by marriage, he was, however, the only Roundhead in his family. He fought in many of the major battles and rose to serve as a colonel under Thomas Fairfax.

In 1647 he was deputed to guard the King whilst he was imprisoned in Hampton Court but allowed him to escape. According to Whalley, this was to foil an assassination attempt on the King. An appointment as one of the judges to try the King followed; he was present throughout the trial and was the fourth signatory on the warrant.

When Cromwell dissolved the Long Parliament, Whalley was deputed to remove 'the Bauble' (the Parliamentary mace). He was appointed as a Major General for Derbyshire, Lincolnshire, Leicestershire, Nottinghamshire and Warwickshire in Cromwell's reorganisation of the country.

Following the Restoration, he left the country for Switzerland, and a price of £100 was put on his head. He sought refuge among the puritan descendants of the Pilgrim Fathers but remained a hunted refugee, hiding in huts, caves and cellars. A romantic story associates his name with Hadley, where the community, surprised by a party of Indians, was losing the fight when the sudden appearance of an elderly man put new heart into the defenders. The legend is that the stranger was Edward Whalley, who had been hiding in the pastor's house. He is thought to have died some time in 1674 or 1675.

11
Lace

When and where lace originated is unknown. A lace-like net dating from around 3000 BC was found in an Egyptian tomb but lace as we know it first appeared in Europe in the fifteenth century. There are two basic types: needlepoint, made with a needle and thread; and bobbin lace, made by twisting and weaving a number of threads in a predetermined pattern. Bobbin lace is held in place during its manufacture by pins which are gradually removed as the work progresses. Lacemaking came to Britain in the sixteenth century and, whereas needlepoint has never been made on a large scale, bobbin lace became an important cottage industry. It became established not only in Devon but also in Buckinghamshire and its neighbouring counties of Bedfordshire and Northamptonshire. This sort of lace is sometimes referred to either as pillow lace, from the large pillow on which the pattern, or parchment, was fixed, or as bone lace, either because the earliest bobbins on which the thread was wound were made of bone, or possibly because fish bones were used as pins when the craft was in its infancy.

The history of machine-made lace also starts in the late sixteenth century, with the invention by William Lee (page 111) of the stocking frame in 1589. Although London was the largest centre of manufacture in the seventeenth century, the East Midlands gradually took over from the capital. While manufacturers in Leicester concentrated on woollen stockings, those in Nottinghamshire began to use cotton or silk and gained experience that stood them in good stead for experiments in adapting the stocking frame to make lace. In 1758 Jedediah Strutt patented the Derby rib machine which made purl ribs on plain stockings. This led the way to a further improvement, patented in 1764 by Thomas and John Morris and John and William Betts, which could make a plain net. Five years later a pattern was introduced in the net by Robert Frost. Frequent and

numerous patents were issued amid much piracy of ideas and other chicanery. A great advance was made in 1786 by John Rogers of Mansfield, who invented 'point net', which would not unravel easily, the main drawback of earlier lace. For the most part any pattern on the lace was made by 'runners', women who worked the needle-run patterns by hand.

Meanwhile the warp frame, said to have been invented by Mr Crane of Edmonton, was being refined to a stage where it superseded the adapted stocking frame and remained in use for much of the nineteenth century. John Heathcote, however, was trying to make lace that was not so much knitted as intertwined like bobbin lace. He patented his twist-net design and machine in 1808 and, using a new cotton thread, was able to produce an improved net at a much reduced cost. When Luddites destroyed his machinery at Loughborough in 1816 he moved the factory to Tiverton in Devon. By 1812 the Pusher machine could make patterned twist-net and in 1813 John Leavers improved Heathcote's invention and gave his name to a type of lace still produced in large quantities today — Leavers lace.

A great advance in the technology of lace machines was made by the use of Jacquard apparatus. Invented in France by Joseph Marie Jacquard in 1801, it was a system of punched cards which regulated the wires determining the pattern, allowing them either to fall through the hole in the card, or to remain in place, where there was no hole in the card. The first patent applying the Jacquard system to a lace machine was taken out by Samuel Draper in 1835. In 1841 Joseph Wragg of Lenton found a way of getting the machine to work with heavier thread outlining the pattern, enabling it to make close copies of bobbin lace and doing away with the need for 'runners' to outline it later by hand. With the advent, in 1846, of John Livesey's lace-curtain machine, making curtains up to 6 feet

(2 metres) wide and 15 feet (4.5 metres) long, and the introduction of steam power, the foundations of the lace trade were firmly in place.

Factories gradually took over from small workshops, although these never entirely died out. Machines ran from 4 am until after midnight, with workers doing two shifts of five hours with a five-hour break in between. Children were employed to wind the thread on to the bobbins: one machine could use up to four thousand bobbins. Women would finish the lace off, splitting the lace borders, which were made side by side, mending, bleaching, dyeing and dressing. Working conditions were appalling, but at least in the boom times there was work. With lace being so dependent on fashion and exporting, there were also times of severe depression, notably the 'Hungry Forties' in the nineteenth century. One of the major employers was Thomas Adams, who was derided for fixing a nine-hour day for his employees, even before the Factory Acts of the 1860s. In addition, he provided a range of facilities for his workers in the factory he built in Stoney Street, Nottingham, in 1855. In the same year another noted manufacturer, Richard Birkin,

built his factory in Broadway. (For a tour incorporating some of the buildings in the Lace Market, see page 99). German-Jewish immigrants were attracted to Nottingham, among them Lewis Heymann, who was one of the instigators of the establishment of the Nottingham School of Design in 1846. They were particularly skilled in exporting as well as manufacturing and by 1900 around 70 per cent of Nottingham lace was sold abroad.

After the First World War the lace industry went into a severe decline. Previously, ladies had worn lace on their dresses, petticoats and bonnets as a matter of course, draped lace shawls over their shoulders and carried lace parasols, but now fashions had irrevocably changed. Although the lace-curtain manufacturers survived, over half the firms making Leavers lace went out of business. Fortunately for the city, the growth of Boots, Players and Raleigh was able to provide new employment. The Raschel lace machine, invented by a German in 1859, was not widely adopted in Nottingham until a century later, and that, together with computer technology, gave a boost to the industry for which the city is still renowned.

A panel of Nottingham lace, showing the Castle, the Council House and Sherwood Forest.

12
Further reading

Beckett, John. *The Book of Nottingham.* Barracuda, 1990.

Brand, Ken. *Thomas Chambers Hine.* Nottingham Civic Society, undated.

Brand, Ken. *Watson Fothergill, Architect.* Nottingham Civic Society, undated.

Brown, Ian. *Nottinghamshire's Industrial Heritage.* Nottinghamshire County Council, 1989.

Brown, Ian. *A Guide to the Civil War in Nottinghamshire.* Nottinghamshire County Council, 1992.

Bradbury, D. J. *Secrets of Sherwood.* Wheel Publications, 1987.

Bryson, Emrys. *Portrait of Nottingham.* Robert Hale, 1983.

Christian, Roy. *Nottinghamshire.* Batsford, 1974.

Earnshaw, Pat. *Lace Machines and Machine Laces.* Batsford, 1986.

Firth, J. B. *Highways and Byways in Nottinghamshire.* Macmillan, 1916.

Halls, Zillah. *Machine-made Lace in Nottingham.* City of Nottingham Museums and Library Committee, 1973.

Hamilton, Andrew. *Nottingham's Royal Castle.* Nottingham Civic Society, undated.

Holt, J. C. *Robin Hood.* Thames & Hudson, 1982.

Kaye, David. *A History of Nottinghamshire.* Phillimore, 1987.

Lawrence, D. H. *Sons and Lovers.* Penguin, 1981.

Marquiss, Richard (editor). *The Nature of Nottinghamshire.* Barracuda, 1987.

Mee, Arthur. *Nottinghamshire.* Hodder & Stoughton, 1938.

Oldfield, Geoffrey. *The Lace Market, Nottingham.* Nottingham Civic Society, undated.

Peters, R. J. *Ancient Bassetlaw.* North Trent Publishing, 1990.

Pevsner, N. (revised by E. Williamson). *Nottinghamshire.* Penguin, 1979.

Roffey, James. *The Chesterfield Canal.* Barracuda, 1989.

Severn, John. *Dovecotes of Nottinghamshire.* Cromwell Press, 1986.

Sillitoe, Alan. *Saturday Night and Sunday Morning.* W. H. Allen, 1958.

Thorold, Henry. *Nottinghamshire.* Faber & Faber, 1984.

Train, Keith. *Twenty Nottinghamshire Families.* Nottinghamshire Local History Council, 1969.

Train, Keith. *Train on Churches.* BBC Radio Nottingham, 1981.

Warner, Tim. *Newark: Civil War and Siegeworks.* Nottinghamshire County Council, 1992.

Weir, Christopher. *A Prospect of Nottinghamshire.* Nottinghamshire Local History Association, 1986.

West, Frank. *Rude Forefathers.* Cromwell Press, 1989.

Wood, A. C. *A History of Nottinghamshire.* SR Publishers, 1971.

13
Tourist information centres

Newark: Gilstrap Centre, Castlegate, Newark NG24 1BG. Telephone: 0636 78962.
Nottingham: 1-4 Smithy Row, Nottingham NG1 2BY. Telephone: 0602 470661.
Nottingham (West Bridgford): County Hall, Loughborough Road, West Bridgford, Nottingham NG2 7QP. Telephone: 0602 823558.
Ollerton: Sherwood Heath, Ollerton Roundabout, Ollerton, Newark NG22 9DR. Telephone: 0623 824545.
Retford: Amcott House Annexe, 40 Grove Street, Retford DN22 6JU. Telephone: 0777 860780.
Sherwood Forest: Visitor Centre, Church Street, Edwinstowe, near Mansfield NG21 9HN. Telephone: 0623 824490.
Trowell: Granada Motorway Services, M1 Northbound, Trowell, Nottingham NG9 3PL. Telephone: 0602 442411.
Worksop: Public Library, Memorial Avenue, Worksop S80 2BP. Telephone: 0909 501148.

14
Tours for motorists

Route 1. Nottingham — Wollaton — Strelley — Awsworth — Eastwood — Brinsley — Annesley — Mansfield — Ravenshead — Newstead Abbey — Papplewick — Bestwood — Nottingham.
Route 2. Nottingham — Clifton — Ratcliffe on Soar — Kingston on Soar — Sutton Bonington — East Leake — Costock — Wysall — Widmerpool — Owthorpe — Cropwell Bishop — Tithby — Bingham — Whatton — Aslockton — Car Colston — East Bridgford — Shelford — Radcliffe on Trent — Holme Pierrepont — Nottingham.
Route 3. Newark — Kelham — Averham — Upton — Southwell — Thurgarton — Gonalston — Lowdham — Epperstone — Oxton — Rufford — Edwinstowe — Ollerton — Wellow — Ompton — Kneesall — Norwell Woodhouse — Norwell — Cromwell — North Muskham — South Muskham — Newark.
Route 4. Mansfield — Sutton in Ashfield — Skegby — Teversal — Mansfield Woodhouse — Warsop — Cuckney — Creswell Crags — Worksop — Clumber — Ollerton — Clipstone — Mansfield.
Route 5. Retford — Welham — Clarborough — Clayworth — Gringley on the Hill — Beckingham — Walkeringham — West Stockwith — Misterton — Gringley on the Hill — Mattersey — Ranskill — Blyth — Oldcotes — Langold — Carlton in Lindrick — Worksop — Ranby — Babworth — Retford.
Route 6. Retford — Clarborough — North and South Wheatley — Sturton-le-Steeple — Littleborough — North Leverton — South Leverton — Treswell — Stokeham — East Drayton — Darlton — Tuxford — Egmanton — Laxton — Moorhouse — Ossington — Carlton-on-Trent — Sutton on Trent — Tuxford — East Markham — Retford.

Index

Page numbers in italic refer to illustrations